HOPE-IN-THE-MIST

Two hundred thirty copies printed :
five copies, lettered A-E, for presentation,
twenty-five copies numbered I-25
specially bound, signed by the authors
and with an original illustration signed by Charles Vess
&
two hundred copies in paper covers

review
copy

HOPE-IN-THE-MIST

The Extraordinary Career
and
Mysterious Life of Hope Mirrlees
by
Michael Swanwick

Preface by
Neil Gaiman

TEMPORARY CULTURE :: 2009

TEMPORARY CULTURE
is published by :
HENRY WESSELLS
P. O. BOX 43072
UPPER MONTCLAIR, NJ 07043

DEDICATION

This book is dedicated to Robin Ian Evelyn Milne Stuart de la Lanne-Mirrlees, Baron of Inchdrewer, Laird of Bernera, Comte de la Lanne, and Prince of Coronata, in gratitude for his passionate championship of his aunt, Hope Mirrlees. Thank you, Robin.

PREFACE

I was, what, eleven ? twelve ? when I read *Lud-in-the-Mist*. I picked it up in the Wilmington Bookshop, in East Grinstead High Street, attracted, I think, by the ethereal cover painting.

It is a book that makes me thirteen again when I read it (although Nathanial Chanticleer was a mystery to me then, and he is not a mystery any more). It is by turns beautiful and wise, a fairy tale and a ghost story (is there really any difference ?) a mystery tale and a Mystery tale, a history of somewhere that does not exist and a portrait of some things that are.

Lud-in-the-Mist comes with many mysteries. In its fusion of genres and styles many mysteries are to be found, and one of the genres it encompasses is that of the detective story, after all. But the edition I read came with an additional mystery — an introduction by Lin Carter. He told us that *Lud-in-the-Mist* was a book that had been printed many years before to no acclaim, but that it had, as good books sometimes do, gathered a band of devotees and become a book that people loved, and that some of the people who loved it had sent him their copies and had insisted he read it for the Ballantine Adult Fantasy Series. Whatever the merits or otherwise of Carter's fiction, his taste as an editor was pretty much impeccable, and he knew quality when he saw it. He talked little about Hope Mirrlees, the author, in his introduction other than to tell us that he could not trace her. He had no idea that she was alive and robust at the time. There was no copyright notice on the book.

In later editions, the Lin Carter introduction was gone and there was a copyright notice. The cover painting was, alas, nowhere near as pretty and ethereal.

I was about nineteen when I first made it into the British Museum Reading Room, that glorious round room that is now the centre of a perfect courtyard and was then surrounded by temporary huts, like a builders site. In one of those huts my photograph was taken, and I was handed my British Library Card. "That'll be ten pounds," said the woman handing me the card, who was very beautiful, and black, and who, when she saw my face fall, panicked, had to reassure me that, no, she had just been joking.

I do not remember how I had managed to get the card. I had written a letter, I know that, telling them, truthfully, I needed books about Caspar Hauser for a play I had decided to write.

Once inside that room, I went wild. I ordered everything they had listed by James Branch Cabell, I remember, all the contemporary accounts of Caspar Hauser's short life and peculiar death they had (and learned many odd things about him. His spittle was adhesive for a start), and everything they had by or about Hope Mirrlees.

You would sit at your place, and people would bring you books. Or sometimes, they would bring you a slip of paper telling you that the book was not in the mysterious stacks, often explaining that, although the book was in the catalogue, it had been destroyed in the blitz.

But soon someone brought me a small, privately printed volume of poems by Hope Mirrlees, *Moods and Tensions*. I was excited. The writing of *Lud-in-the-Mist* is musical. Her rewrite of the Fool's Song sits in the back of my head always. She was a poet. And I read her poems puzzled and slightly numb, unable to find anything of the author of *Lud-in-the-Mist* there. There were lines in the book that had been crossed out and rewritten in pencil by, I assumed, Hope Mirrlees herself. (Later in life I would buy, at different times, two different versions of this pamphlet of poems. In each edition, different lines were crossed out and replaced by the author.)

In the same way, some years later, my delight at finding, fifteen years ago, in a bookhop in Stillwater, *A Fly in Amber,* her first volume of biography of antiquarian Sir Robert Cotton, was replaced by dejected fascination. Each sentence felt like a palimpsest, written and rewritten so many times that only the author knew any longer what sense she had originally meant to convey. Reading it was the literary experience of wading through glue : fine glue, but glue nonetheless. The novel *The Counterplot* was unimpressive (although competent for what it was). *The Book of the Bear* was well-retold folk stories. I can understand someone accidentally writing a good book, and being unable to repeat it. I could not understand someone capable of writing a book that good, that wise, that elegant, and unable to write anything else in which a reader could take pleasure. It was a mystery.

Hope Mirrlees. Who was she? And why, why just that one book ? Why nothing before to show she was capable of it, why nothing afterwards with the same glimmer of beauty, the same air of competence and good sense, the same clear, wise, pristine, uncluttered writing ?

I was too lazy to do anything more than wonder.

Fortunately Michael Swanwick is not similarly lazy. He

was haunted by the same questions that haunted me, and set off in search of answers. Along the way he points out how deeply *Lud-in-the-Mist* is built out of the bricks of English folklore and fairylore, and he paints a portrait of a woman and her world.

As with *Lud-in-the-Mist*, Michael Swanwick gives us answers, but he does not give us all the answers ; the mysteries of the woman and her book are never entirely dispelled ; but still and withal, like the promise of fairy fruit, he gives us hope.

Neil Gaiman
Flying Home from Boston, 24 April 2009

HOPE-IN-THE-MIST

H ope Mirrlees is easily the most mysterious of the great twentieth-century fantasists. She wrote one important work of modern fantasy, *Lud-in-the-Mist*, and then abruptly fell into silence. Her single professionally published poem was only the fifth work put out by Leonard and Virginia Woolf's Hogarth Press, and is considered by critics to be a significant and possibly even important modernist work. But, despite her long and enduring friendship with T. S. Eliot, she never followed it up. She was a fringe member of the twentieth century's single most prestigious literary sorority, the Bloomsbury group, and yet by 1970 she was almost completely forgotten. There are no biographies of her, few pictures, and personal information is dauntingly difficult to find. The mists of time have closed around her.

Still, traces remain. With patience, it is possible to gather together these widely-scattered references to Mirrlees, and so assemble a rough sketch of her life and achievements.

Let this slim book serve as a beginning.

H elen Hope Mirrlees (dropping first names in favor of the middle was something of a tradition in her family) was born in Chislehurst, Kent, on April 8, 1887, the daughter of Emily Lina Moncrieff and William Julius Mirrlees,[1] a wealthy industrialist. From the very beginning, she was a woman who knew her own mind.

Explaining why relatives affectionately called her "appalling," her cousin once removed, Catriona Kelly, recalled a family story :

> . . . wandering round a garden with her grandmother, known as 'Ga', who was rather a fey kind of person, when the latter pointed out some trees and said : 'Oh look, Hopie, lovely trees, would not Hopey like to climb those lovely trees' Hope replied (aged three) : 'Ga climb trees self', which my mother said was always told to her as an illustration of the awfulness of Hope, but my mother herself found rather admirable.[2]

The Mirrlees family had been on the rise for quite some time.[3] Hope's grandfather, James Buchanan Mirrlees, was an enormously successful manufacturer of sugar-refining equipment, who later branched out into other large machinery. Mirrlees Blackstone is still prominent as a manufacturer of diesel engines. William Julius,[4] the oldest son of eleven children, was very much in his father's mold, an inventive man with a lively interest in everything. He trained in Glasgow as an engineer, and then made his own fortune in South Africa, as part owner and part founder of Tongaat-Hulett, today the eighth-largest sugar company in the world. As a result, Mirrlees grew up accustomed to exclusive schools, frequent travel, and motor-cars as birthday presents.[5] Her father set up generous trust funds for all his children, so that they would never be in need. When adversity came into her life, this last fact was to prove her undoing.

Lina Mirrlees was born a Moncrieff, and the Moncrieffs were old, landed aristocracy.[6] In later life, Hope was to boast that she was descended from Scottish royalty on her mother's side, and though this was of a piece with her self-characterization as a "poetess," it is verifiably so. Certainly it loomed large in her imagination.

Lina and Julius saw three of their six children survive to adulthood. Hope was their eldest. After her came William Henry Buchanan, later a major-general and a close friend and confidant to King Edward VIII. Margaret Rosalys, known to all as Margot, was the youngest. Later living with Hope's mother was Miss Constance Sarah Louisa Moncrieff, a maiden aunt known to the family as Aunt Cockie.[7] When, as an adult, Hope fell seriously ill with typhoid, her parents rushed to Seville to care for her.

2

When she needed a place to live, she was always welcome home. Virginia Woolf once had dinner with the family at the Rubens Hotel, and thought them an archetypal warm-hearted British family, of a sort untouched in any way by the previous hundred years. "I wonder whether its natural for families to keep together," she mused. "I didn't wonder, though, that night. Unlimited silver flowed out of Sneezer's pockets."[8]

Hope grew up partly in Scotland, partly in England, with frequent stays in South Africa. "Hope had a black nanny and could speak fluent Zulu," her nephew reported. "She taught me a song in Zulu which I still remember, and I tried it out on the black porter of a hotel. He said 'It's quite innocent and just means "I love my black nanny because she is so good to me." ' or words to that effect."[9] She was educated at home by French governesses (all her life, people were to comment on the perfection of her spoken French) until, at the age of eleven, she entered the Besires School as a boarder. This was followed by St. Andrews Preparatory School, and then St. Leonards in St. Andrews. She disliked the first two schools, but loved the third, chiefly, she later said, for the friendships and camaraderie she enjoyed there.

Her first ambition was to be an actress, and to this end she enrolled in the Royal Academy of Dramatic Art. By her own testimony, however, she played truant by going to the British Museum to hear lectures on Greek Art (ever since her father had read Kingsley's Heroes to her as a child, she had wanted to learn Greek),[10] and was lost to the theater forever. In 1910, she entered Newnham College[11] to read Classics, and her true story began.

Hope Mirrlees was a strikingly beautiful young woman. She had a chalk white face, jet black hair, and violet eyes. She dressed outrageously, like a gypsy, in sequins and gold, with silk scarves and amber necklaces cascading down from her neck. Men — academic men in particular — found her entrancing. "In Hope would dart like a humming-bird, towards the end of a lesson, her sapphire eyes flashing, her pendant earrings swinging ; a soft torrent of musical sounds issuing from her lips," wrote one admirer, who also called her, "a cross between a pixy and a genius."[12] Another later reminisced, "Over fifty years ago Miss Hope Mirrlees bowled me over, first by the beauty of her bearing and cerulean eyes, a minute later by her dulcet voice, and next by the charming acuteness of her talk ; never previously had I met so seductive a bluestocking."[13]

Virginia Woolf was less susceptible to her charms. "She is her own heroine — capricious, exacting, exquisite, very learned and beautifully dressed,"[14] Woolf wrote when feeling generous, and declared her "eccentric impulsive ecstatic odd,"[15] when not. She characterized Mirrlees as "a very self conscious, wilful, prickly & perverse young woman, rather conspicuously well dressed & pretty, with a view of her own about books & style, an aristocratic & conservative tendency in opinion, & a corresponding taste for the beautiful & elaborate in literature," and declared her to be no more governable than a flock of bright green parakeets.[16] On another event, she wrote, "but the affectations of that young woman !"[17] and deemed her beauty obnoxious. Nevertheless, she considered Mirrlees to be a friend, and frequently urged her to write a story, a play, poems — anything ! — for the Hogarth Press.[18]

If Hope Mirrlees was an aristocratic young woman, she came by it honestly. At age nineteen or twenty, as a matter of course, she was presented to the court as a debutante. Her family had that sort of wealth and position.

Moreover, she was extremely intelligent and possibly even brilliant. She spoke several languages fluently.[19] She knew all the intellectual lights of her time, flitting inconsequently through the lives and sometimes biographies of Gertrude Stein, Bertrand Russell, André Gide, Lady Ottoline Morrell, Anthony Powell, Walter de la Mare, Arthur Waley, Katharine Mansfield, Roger Fry, Pablo Picasso, Somerset Maugham, William Butler Yeats, T.S. Eliot, and more significantly through the life of the classicist Jane Ellen Harrison, with whom she shared apartments.

For a few brief years, Mirrlees shone bright as a candle flame. Her first novel came out in 1919, and through the 1920s she published a respectable array of novels, essays, poetry, and translations. She got attention, she got reviews, she got praise. Then, shortly after publication of her most successful work, the fantasy novel *Lud-in-the-Mist*, the flame guttered out. She put on weight, lost her looks, ceased writing, focused all her attention on her pug dog and her thyroid gland, and fell into obscurity. These events Woolf chronicled in a scattering of brief but vivid paragraphs in her diaries and letters. Taken together, these entries form a sad and cautionary tale. They are, however, like all such tales, at least in part a work of fiction.

In 1910 Hope Mirrlees enrolled in Classics at Newnham College, Cambridge University. A college for women was no longer the curiosity it was when Newnham opened in 1875. But a university education was still a rare privilege for a young woman, and a good indication of how well-off and indulgent her parents were.[20]

At Newnham, Mirrlees studied under the guidance of the woman who was to be the single greatest influence on her life, Jane Ellen Harrison.

Jane Ellen Harrison (1850-1928), Greek scholar and Lecturer in Classical Archaeology at Newnham 1898 to 1922, was the author of influential books, most notably *Prologomena to the Study of Greek Religion* and *Themis* ; famed as one of the "Cambridge Ritualists" ; and a woman whose theories on the origins of art from chthonic religions hold sway even today. Mary Beard characterized her as "the most famous female classicist there has ever been, an originary and radical thinker, a permanent fixture in the history of scholarship."[21] Her thoughts on religion, ritual, and ecstasy were to provide the theoretical underpinnings for all three of Hope's novels as well as her one major poem.

Harrison's first biographer, Jessie Stewart, implied that Mirrlees met Harrison through Hope's parents, who were the older woman's friends. However, she also referred to Hope's parents as "Mr. Willey Mirrlees and his wife Lena, 'the adored "Maffey," ' "[22] when in fact, the father was called Julius or WJ by his friends, but never Willey, and Lina's actual nickname was Mappie. She also started Mirrlees at Newnham a year earlier than the facts justified. Given how often Stewart was wrong on such matters, it is equally possible that the lecturer at the British Museum whose siren call lured Hope away from the theater was in fact Jane.[23] However they met, the two women had a friendly student-and-mentor correspondence going by the time she decided to enroll in Newnham.

In 1910 Hope broke up her engagement to "some young captain or other,"[24] of whom almost no trace — not even his name — remains. This mysterious young captain surfaced briefly as a character in Mirrlees' first two novels, and then disappeared forever and without a trace. As portrayed in *Madeleine* and *The Counterplot*, he was intelligent (though in neither case up to the standards of her demanding heroines), attentive, and cheerfully level-headed. He was, in short, the sort of suitor my female friends would dismissively refer to as a "nice young man." Nice young men have never done well with beautiful young bluestockings. Perhaps it was just as well. Ninety years after the fact, Hope's nephew, in a letter of fond reminiscences, remarked, "Hope would have made a terrible wife and a heartless mother, in spite of all her talents, or rather, because of her talents. She was not at all interested in practical things or settling down in one place."[25]

While at the RADA, Mirrlees later claimed, she was the *protégée* of Mrs. Patrick Campbell. If so, this left a greater impression on Hope than on the famed actress, for a quick scan of the standard biographies reveals no reference to Mirrlees. She obviously had, however, a natural instinct for endearing herself to mentors, for she quickly became Jane Harrison's favorite.

Immediately upon leaving Newnham in 1913, Mirrlees went to

Paris with a college friend, Karin Costelloe, to study and write.[26] With this, Mirrlees began (or possibly continued) a lifelong pattern of root-lessness, vacillating between Cambridge and Paris, with frequent travel in between. Karin Costelloe soon married Adrian Stephen, Virginia Woolf's brother, giving Hope entree into the Bloomsbury group.

Sometime in this period, Hope and Jane began intermittently rooming together. On October 13, 1914, Harrison wrote from Paris, "We are going to the Embassy to see if we can get permits for the front to see Hope Mirrlees' brother."[27] In 1915 the two returned to Paris to visit Harrison's heart doctor and, discovering the Ecole des Langues Orientales around the corner from their hotel, decided to stay and study Russian. A great advantage to living together for both ladies was that, at the time, it was simply not respectable for a single woman to travel alone.

In Paris, Hope waded knee-deep in dreams, gazed down from her top floor rooms in the Hôtel de l'Elysée at street venders and black-shawled women carrying long loaves in the narrow rue de Beaune, sought out the Île Saint-Louis, the rue Saint Antoine, the Place des Vosges, where the seventeenth century still lay exquisitely dying. She and Jane went to Benediction in Notre-Dame-des-Champs. She studied the art in the Louvre, saw the ghost of Père Lachaise walking the streets, cata-logued the smells of the Grands Boulevards (cloacae, hot india rubber, poudre de riz, Algerian tobacco), saw the whores like lions seeking their meat from God, read *Crime and Punishment*, stayed up all night talking, talking, talking.

Paris was, in fine, everything a young woman of intellectual bent could desire of a city.

It is possible to be young and literary and yet not at all bohemi-an. That year, Virginia Woolf's friend, David "Bunny" Garnett, who was staying in an attic room at the same hotel as Mirrlees,[28] heard that D.H. Lawrence's new novel, *The Rainbow*, had been burned by the police. He burst out to Hope, whom he had never met before, upon the iniquity of burning books. As Woolf later related, "She was so much of his way of thinking that he exclaimed 'You darling !' — & offended her — although, as he explained, he was on the far side of the room, & used the word 'darling' in its other sense. I suppose he never had a rich vocabu-lary."[29] Hope hinted he ought to be in the army.

In ways Hope was a conventional and even a timid woman. Anthony Powell, in *Faces in My Time*, relates how, decades later in 1944, he and his wife had Hope Mirrlees and Colonel Kalla, a Czech military attaché, to lunch. While they were having drinks, Kalla abruptly fixed a steady gaze upon Mirrlees and slowly began to advance upon her, as if overcome by sudden love. Hope was terrified. "She straightened her somewhat dumpy figure in readiness for the final pounce," Powell recorded. "Kalla's deliberate advance continued. Waiting for the climax imposed an agonizing strain. When he stopped there was a rapid movement. His hand shot out towards the bare neck of Hope Mirrlees.

"'Ladies are sometimes frightened of these.'

"With a courtliness of gesture, recalling his own military beginnings as an officer of the long departed Dual Monarchy of clicking heels and Strauss waltzes, Kalla removed an earwig from her scarf."[30]

Were Hope and Jane lovers ? This is a question that many have weighed in on, with very little evidence one way or the other. In a letter, Woolf wrote of Mirrlees that, "we like seeing her and Jane billing and cooing together."[31] Coming from anyone else, this would be conclusive. But Woolf, as shall be shown, was not always a reliable witness.

Evidence almost as strong is provided by Harrison's biographer, Sandra Peacock, who wrote : "Hope proved her fidelity early on when she broke off her engagement to a young man in 1910. The man's name and the actual circumstances of their engagement have never surfaced, but it is known that Jane approved of Hope's action and rejoiced over her return to Newnham. In a letter postmarked July 3, 1910, Jane sent her condolences on the breakup, saying she was 'relieved it is ended — for tho' "pedestrian love" is a good & great thing it is not quite enough I think on which to climb the steep stair of marriage.' "[32]

But Mary Beard, in her meta-biography *The Invention of Jane Harrison*, establishes that this smoking gun was achieved by leaving out most of the note. Partially restored, it reads as follows :

Thank you for writing to tell me about yr engagement. I am relieved it is ended — for tho' 'pedestrian love' is a good & great thing —it is not quite enough I think on which to climb the steep stair of marriage. Anyhow I am truly glad we shall have you at Newnham next autumn . . . We must scheme out a course of work before term begins — but for the present you have enough in the *Odyssey*.[33]

Which sounds less like a note from a jealous lover than the sort of thing a conscientious teacher would write to a valued student.

Reading *Madeleine* for review, Woolf commented, "It's all sapphism so far as I've got — Jane and herself,"[34] which, insofar as anybody cares about that novel nowadays, has become the conventional wisdom — that the passionate (and expressly lesbian) yearning of Madeleine for Mademoiselle de Scudéry, though Platonic and unrequited, reflected Hope's feelings for Jane. Yet Mademoiselle de Scudéry as portrayed therein — self-centered, judgmental, and completely artificial — has nothing to do with the Jane Ellen Harrison who charmed so many and was capable of writing, "We cannot all be distinguished. But for heaven's sake let us all be shabby and comfortable."[35]

In fact, as Julia Briggs pointed out in a review in the *London Review of Books*,[36] Harrison appears in the book as Mere Agnes Arnault, the Mother Superior of the Abbaye of Port-Royale, who kindly tries to dissuade Madeleine from her self-destructive course. "Her face, slightly tanned and covered with clear, fine wrinkles . . . gave her the look of one of the Holy Women in a picture by Mantegna. Her hazel eyes were clear and liquid and child-like."[37] Once again, the supposed evidence crumbles underfoot.

Mirrlees' nephew wrote the dissenting opinion : "So was Hope homosexual ? No, definitely not, but I think she pretended to be ! I mean it was the fashion in those days, because about 100 years ago Oscar Wilde had set the trend. But the fact is that Hope never got married, and I think some very young man had a merciful escape."[38]

Ironically enough, the question arises perennially because of the contents of the Harrison Archive at Newnham College, which Mirrlees herself assembled and then culled. Martha Vicinus went through the archive and found that many of Harrison's friends, thinking Mirrlees far too possessive of Harrison's life and feeling excluded from it, accused her of homoerotic feelings toward Harrison. "HM herself was known for her female friendships, and she speaks quite passionately about her own private, personal knowledge of JEH, which makes her the only possible biographer of JEH, but also makes it impossible for her to write candidly about her. Of course, all this is innuendo, but pretty strongly stated."[39]

Even more damaging to the reputations of both ladies is the archive's preservation of their private correspondence. They had, it seems, a rich fantasy life involving their many cuddly toys and knick-knacks, centering on The Great Bear (aka Ursa Major, Herr Bear, and the Old One), a stuffed animal given Harrison by Helen Verral, one of her students at Newnham, when the teddy-bear first became popular in 1906.[40] Hope was known as the "Younger Walrus" and Jane as the "Elder Walrus," and the Bear was husband to them both. A typical note invites Mirrlees to join Harrison for dinner and student theatricals : "I desire that my young Wife do dine in Hall tomorrow with my elder Wife and go to the young ladies Revue. I desire that my elder wife do not dragnet my younger wife the whole evening. She is not a comic cut she is my young wife. Given in the Cave – in the presence of Mrs. Mutz and the Glass Horse."[41] The note was signed with the pattern of the constellation Ursa Major. "The Cave" was Jane's room in Newnham.

On another occasion, Harrison wrote, "The Bear (his temperature is lower but he is still very weak) sends Mr. Velvet Brown with his compliments to stay with you till you are better."[42] The original Mr. Velvet Brown was a cat belonging to Harrison's nephew, of which Harrison wrote, " 'Mr. Velvet Brown' played a large part in the home life of the Vicarage, which he never left till death removed him. He was a cat of great dignity. Tail in air, he always trotted after my brother-in-law on his parish rounds."[43] In Greece, Harrison had found, in a pile of rubble at the Acropolis Museum, a carving of a she-bear which she identified as a totem of Artemis Brauronia. All well-born Athenian girls had to accomplish their *bear-service* before they could marry. They, as she, felt a special reverence for the Great She-Bear. One of two significant dreams in Harrison's life was of bears dancing in the woods. She tried to teach them a formal dance, failed, and finally realized that their shambling dance was beautiful and that she was there not to teach but to learn from them. She woke up crying, in an ecstasy of humility.

All of which serves as an indication of the richness in associative value these notes had for their participants. But it was a mistake for Mirrlees to preserve them, for they are so coy and twee that they uniformly aggravate all the researchers who have to deal with them. Many have concluded that the Bear represented the two women's symbolic marriage.

This may or may not be true. To be twee is not necessarily to be gay. It is worth noting that the first biography of Harrison was based on her letters to her friend and fellow Oxford Ritualist Professor Gilbert Murray that were almost as cloying and in-jokish as those to Mirrlees, and that his wife expressed concern that they would make both the principals look foolish if published.

Harrison herself referred to Mirrlees as "my pupil and friend,"[44] and wrote in *Reminiscences of a Student's Life*, "I admit, Fate has been very kind to me. In my old age she has sent me, to comfort me, a ghostly daughter dearer than any child after the flesh."[45] (There was a 37-year disparity between their ages ; Jane was ten years older than Hope's father.) Hope presented their relationship as a passionate friendship — profound but, by implication, sexless. Their friend, Professor E.M. Butler, in a similar vein, said, "There was a natural affinity between them, dissimilar though they were in many ways, neither remotely resembling anyone else in the world."[46]

The two ladies would doubtless have been horrified to find their sexual orientation a matter of public debate. But though there is no lack of strongly-voiced opinions, in the final analysis there is no definite proof one way or another. In the end, whatever one decides is, at base, a sentimental choice.

In July 1914, Gertrude Stein and Alice B. Toklas, who needed to see Stein's London publisher, accepted an invitation, arranged by Hope, to spend ten days at Cambridge with Mrs. Mirrlees. Gertrude liked the food, the weather, and the house. Alice had harsh words to say about English breakfasts. They went to Newnham to meet Jane Harrison, but did not find her particularly interesting. Lina Mirrlees threw them several dinner parties. Of one, Toklas later wrote :

> At the Mirrlees' one night, we met Dr. Alfred North Whitehead and Mrs. Whitehead. After dinner he asked me if he could take me to the garden where we would have coffee. I did not know who he was at the time, and only when I saw his face under a lamp did I recognize him. He had a most benign sweet smile and a simplicity that comes only in geniuses. He was my third genius for whom the bell rang. The other two had been Gertrude Stein and Picasso.[47]

Which establishes that Mirrlees had, from early on, excellent literary connections in Paris, a fact that would have gone unrecorded had not Toklas been so taken with Dr. Whitehead.

Her connections in London were also excellent. In 1918, either through the literary salonist Lady Ottoline Morrell[48] (Mirrlees would, on Morrell's death, be named one of her literary executors) or by intercession of her old college chum, Mirrlees met a woman who was to have relatively little effect upon her life, but a great deal on how she would be remembered : Virginia Woolf. The very first mention of Mirrlees in Woolf's diaries, that of August 24, sets the tone that would dominate their relationship : "She [Karin Stephen] informs me that I with my tastes would have much in common with Hope Mirrlees ; 'with my tastes' indeed !"[49] By September, however, she had asked Hope to write a story for her and Leonard's dining-room table publishing house, Hogarth Press. In January of the next year, she included Hope in a short list of her friends.

To be a friend, of course, is also to quarrel. Within the month, Woolf wrote Vanessa Bell, "I'm afraid I've quarrelled with Katherine Mansfield and Mirrlees ; which makes me think that these young women with all their charm are as brittle as barley sugar."[50] But the falling-out was imaginary. A week later she wrote, "Well, I haven't even quarrelled with Mirrlees — my literary ladies are faithful, though intermittent, whether purposely or not, I don't undertake to say."[51]

If Virginia was not the easiest of friends, neither was Hope. A month later, Woolf recounted seeing Mirrlees off on her return to Paris :

'Will you write to me, Hope ?' I asked.

'O no. I can't write to people.'

So we parted in the Charing Cross Road for the next six months, I suppose.[51]

It's a moment that, with benefit of hindsight, makes a writer want to stand up in the cinema of the imagination and shout at the screen. To be a member of the Bloomsbury group is to have one's career perennially up for reassessment, to be always given just one more shot at immortality. Nor are there many literary figures whose letters are so constantly examined or ready of access as are Woolf's. Refusing to enter into correspondence with her was a career blunder of the first magnitude.

Still, how could Hope have known ? The two women were not exactly simpatico. On Friday August 8, 1919, Hope Mirrlees arrived at Hogarth House for a long weekend to discuss her poems. She made a definite impression. The day after she left, Virginia wrote to a friend, characterizing Hope as "a capricious young woman, but rather an exquisite apparition, scented, powdered, dressing for dinner, and very highly cultivated."[53] A week later, more composed, she related the whole story to yet another friend :

Last weekend, however, we had a young lady who changed her dress every night for dinner — which Leonard and I cooked ; the servants being on holiday. Her stockings matched a wreath in her hair ; every night they were differently colored ; powder fell about in flakes ; and the scent was such we had to sit in the garden. Moreover, she knows Greek and Russian better than I do French ; is Jane Harrison's favorite pupil, and has written a very obscure, indecent, and brilliant poem, which we are going to print. It's a shame that all this should be possible to the younger generation ; still, I feel something must be lacking, don't you?[54]

Exasperated and yet, in spite of herself, impressed, she agreed to put out something by Mirrlees. Early the next year, in May, 1920, Leonard and Virginia Woolf published Hope's "obscure, indecent and brilliant" poem *Paris* as a 23-page hand-set chapbook in an edition of 175 copies. Aggressively modern, it began :

I want a holophrase
NORD-SUD
ZIG-ZAG
LION NOIR
CACAO BLOOKER
Black-figured vases in Etruscan tombs
RUE DU BAC (DUBONNET)
SOLFERINO (DUBONNET)
CHAMBRE DES DEPUTES
Brekekekek coax coax we are passing under the Seine
DUBONNET

Nord-Sud is an underground railway connecting Montparnasse and Montmartre, and also the name of a Dadaist journal edited by Pierre Reverdy. The other words in caps are posters and stations. The nonsense phrase, "Brekekekek coax coax," evocative of subways wheels clacking on rails, is actually part of the chorus from Aristophanes' *The Frogs*. The black-figured Etruscan vases were an area of particular expertise for Harrison, and "I want a holophrase" alludes to her discussion of early language in *Themis*. Here, the holophrase (literally, a single word that expresses a whole phrase or combination of ideas) is the poem itself, embodying Paris in a voyage that begins with a fearful descent into the underground, wanders through past and present, and ends with the sun rising after a joyful sleepless night, with somewhere the President of the Republic lying in bed beside his wife, babies being born in the Abbaye of Port-Royal, and the sky saffron behind the two towers of Notre-Dame. It concludes with an exuberant JE VOUS SALUE PARIS PLEIN DE GRACE[55] and the Sign of the Bear with which Hope signed all her novels :

3 Rue de Beaune
Paris
Spring 1919

It is easier to explain the poem line by line than it is to judge it as a whole. Like many modernist works, it encodes a great deal of material, both personal and public, in very little space. Julia Briggs, who considered *Paris* Mirrlees' masterpiece, agreed with Woolf's reading of it as an implicit lesbian love poem, but also saw it as being "terrifically engaged with the post-war moment, the strike in Paris of I May 1919, the demobbed soldiers, President Wilson arriving for the Treaty of Versailles etc etc — also an elegy for the dead, also an assertion of solidarity with the French, and the French avant-garde at that."[56] For the common reader, a trot sheet would be useful. Nevertheless, even on the most superficial level, it is a charming and graceful work, and long exposure to it has convinced me that Ms Briggs' enthusiasm was entirely justified.[57]

There are, moreover, critics who believe that *Paris* was an influence on T.S. Eliot's *The Waste Land*.[58]

Certainly, the timing is right. The one poem prefigured the other by three years, just enough time to be absorbed by Eliot, percolate through his poetic sensibility, and emerge transformed. His own Hogarth Press chapbook, *Poems*, immediately preceded *Paris*, so the Woolfs would almost certainly have given him a copy of Mirrlees' poem. But like all the great fantasists of the twentieth century, Mirrlees is seriously out of step with her times. While it does recognize the ills of the age, *Paris* is bright with joy and a marvelous appreciation of beauty and of the past. Coming right after the horrors of World War I, it is almost willful in its rejection of the Zeitgeist.

15

If Mirrlees was an influence on Eliot, it was not as an origina-
tor but as a carrier of French surrealist techniques to the English poet.
In later years, she admitted that *Paris* was "liberated, so to speak, came
to life, owing to a poem by Cocteau called *Le Cape de Bonne Espérance*."[59]
Doubt is cast even on that role, however, by the fact that Eliot, who
was a loyal and kindly friend to her, never publicly acknowledged any
such literary debt. In a laudatory essay on *The Counterplot*, Charles Du
Bos stated that in retrospect the mature work of the novel had enabled
him to appreciate virtues in *Paris* which were not immediately apparent
to him on first reading because it was like so many similar works being
written by young people across Europe at that time.[60] Late in life,
Mirrlees herself wrote that, "I never discussed *Paris* with [Eliot] and I
am unaware whether he ever saw it."[61] Still, the books are not closed
on this issue. It is entirely possible that the case will yet be made and
proven.

Moreover, Julia Briggs has persuasively argued that the then-
experimental use of white space in Virginia Woolf's *Jacob's Room* was
inspired not (as is usually assumed) by Eliot, whose work in 1919 still
followed conventional forms, but by Mirrlees :

> . . . it was Hope Mirrlees' typographically highly experimen-
> tal poem *Paris* that introduced her to the significance of the
> spaces on the page. Three accidentally surviving pages in proof
> with detailed instructions on lay-out from Mirrlees indicate
> just how difficult that task was, suggesting, moreover, that
> Mirrlees may have played a larger part than has previously been
> supposed in Woolf's turn to modernism. Very little of their
> correspondence has survived, but when Hope wrote to con-
> gratulate Virginia on *Jacob's Room*, she responded with an expec-
> tation of understanding — "I don't feel satisfied that I have
> brought it off. Writing without the old bannisters, one makes
> jumps and jerks that are not necessary."[62]

Beyond its importance as a poem, *Paris* demonstrates that the
evocative prose of *Lud-in-the-Mist* did not arise out of nothing. There are
passages, mingling sensuality with mythology, to which any fantasist will
resonate :

The Seine, old egotist, meanders imperturbably towards the sea
Ruminating on weeds and rain . . .

   If through his sluggish waters sleep come dreams
   They are the blue ghosts of king-fishers.

and, in a more theoretical vein :

                    Stories . . .
              The lost romance
        Penned by some Ovid, an unwilling thrall
                 In Fairyland
             No one knows its name ;
    It was the guild-secret of the Italian painters.
     They spent their lives in illustrating it. . . .
      The Chinese village in a genius's mind. . . .
      Little funny things ceaselessly happening.

The poem received mixed reviews. *The Athenaeum* was appreciative. But a brief bug-squisher in the May 6 *Times Literary Supplement* harrumphed, "It seems meant by a sort of futurist trick to give an ensemble of the sensations offered to a pilgrim through Paris. But it is certainly not a 'Poem,' though we follow the author's guidance in classing it as such. To print the words 'there is no lily of the valley' in a vertical column of single letters might be part of a nursery game. It does not belong to the art of poetry." Nor did it sell. Twelve days later, Woolf noted in her diary that though Hope still dribbled along, she was a negligible matter.

The poem has weaknesses. A prudish slap at Freud and two pieces of casual racism, a "Jap" and a "nigger," both meant to be breezily jazzy,[63] display glaring lapses of thought. Still, at the very least, it was an extremely promising beginning. And if the speculations of the critics are correct, it may have been an important influence on the single most famous poem of the twentieth century.

She never wrote anything remotely like it again.

Even more puzzling, though for the rest of her life she insisted on identifying herself as a poetess, she would not publish another poem for over forty years.

The poem was a passing incident in a busy life. Far more important to Mirrlees was her first novel. In 1919, after years of work, she finally published *Madeleine, One of Love's Jansenists*. The best summation of its plot was provided by Hope Mirrlees herself, in an interview in 1970 :

> Madeleine Toqueville is the only child of bourgeois parents of slender means. They live in the provinces. The period is the middle of the seventeenth century.
>
> Madeleine, who has a certain ethereal beauty is deeply read in the literature of the day and is a humble worshipper at a distance of the Parisian *Précieuses* who were to be Molière's butt in his *Précieuses Ridicules*. In 1554 the family move to Paris, and Madeleine is possessed by the desire to become an habituée of the salon of Madame de Rambouillet who is the queen of the Précieuses. Madeleine's wishful thinking expresses itself in a sort of neurosis. She dances up & down the room imagining her entree to Madame de R.'s salon and creating word for word all the conversation that takes place. The conversation is based on those of the popular precious romances of the day, specially those of Mademoiselle de Scudéry. They are elaborate, heavy and extremely tiresome (Madeleine in her reconstructions of them, outshines, of course, everyone else). I spare the reader *nothing.* . . .64

To which can be added that the years of research and learning that went into the book weigh very heavily on it indeed, that the expositions of Jansenism (a dour Roman Catholic philosophy that Madeleine rather perversely attempts to wed to the world view of *Les Précieuses*) are wearying in the extreme, and that — and here is the fault that sinks the work — Madeleine herself is absolutely without redeeming qualities. Nor is this simply a case of Mirrlees unwittingly revealing her own shortcomings in a work of autobiographical fiction. Every petulant snub and self-absorbed vanity of the character is heavily underscored by the author, as if she were afraid the reader might miss the inherent unpleasantness of her protagonist.

Perhaps Hope was exploring, in grotesquely exaggerated form, tendencies she found deplorable in her younger self. Perhaps she simply spent so many years writing and rewriting the novel (and suffering several rejections in the process) that she unconsciously set out to sabotage it. Whatever the reason, the author's loathing for her own protagonist makes for tedious reading. At the end of the book, Madeleine dances off into the void of madness.[65] But since her fatal flaw is simple immaturity, she is neither so monstrous as to make her downfall enjoyable nor sympathetic enough for it to elicit pity.

Nevertheless, *Madeleine* is transparently a *roman à clef*, with Hope herself in the title role, a loving but hapless mother, a father who is a figure of fun and unfaithful to his wife, a mischievous old woman who is clearly her Aunt Cockie, an even-tempered young man who is an echo of her mysterious captain, and Jane Ellen Harrison as a wise old nun who tries to save Madeleine from her own folly. That leaves the role of Madame de Scudéry unfilled, but perhaps there was no original for her. Where the other characters feel like badly-made caricatures, she is an abstraction, someone who might have stepped directly from one book to another. It may be that the original of Madame de Scudéry was Madame de Scudéry, just as another character in the novel, Madame Poilou, was a historical personage of the era.

Julia Briggs has written that "*Madeleine* is a *roman à clef*, recording its author's disappointment with Nathalie Barney and her circle of latter-day *précieuses*,"[66] and elsewhere that "Mme de Scudéry is probably a lightly disguised portrait of Nathalie Barney, the Sappho of her day ; she may well have snubbed Hope as Mme de Scudéry snubs Madeleine."[67] Certainly Barney's literary circle would have been unavoidable to any young woman of serious literary bent living in Paris at that time — most particularly if that young woman were, as many suspected and her novel very strongly hinted, a lesbian. Unhappily, Briggs did not live long enough to prove her case. It is possible that the novel is a satire of 1920s Parisian — or Parisian "Sapphist" — literary life or even (but this is a stretch) of the Bloomsbury set. Even if it is, though, it is not a particularly interesting satire.

Mirrlees provided a short introduction, explaining her intentions. "Life," she wrote, "is like a blind and limitless expanse of sky, for ever dividing into tiny drops of circumstance that rain down, thick and fast, on the just and unjust alike. Art is like the dauntless plastic force that builds up stubborn, amorphous substance cell by cell, into the frail geometry of a shell." And later, "In the outer world there is nothing but the ceaseless, meaningless drip of circumstances, in the inner world — a silent, ineluctable march towards a predestined climax."[68] This, however ineptly embodied in the novel itself, is Mirrlees' great theme : the tension between life and art, between reality and fantasy, between the world as it is, and the world as we would have it be.

The book was dedicated simply "To My Mother."

For all its faults, *Madeleine* was Hope's first novel ; it had taken years to write and been rejected by six or seven publishers before it finally saw life. So she was hurt when Virginia Woolf — who had earlier provided advice on how to get the book published — gave it a review in the *Times Literary Supplement* that could be best characterized as baffled and kind. "From her preface . . . it is evident that Miss Hope Mirrlees is unusually aware of both the difficulties and of the possibilities of the art of fiction," Woolf wrote, grappling for something nice to say. "That is at once something gained ; to be aware of a difficulty may not mean that you solve it, but it does imply an intelligent choice." Further in, she commented, "the success of Madeleine, if not complete, is sufficient to show that Miss Mirrlees has grasped her problem with exceptional firmness." Finally, she concluded that "it is well worth while to read this difficult and interesting novel."[69]

Nevertheless, the book was respectfully received. In a letter, Katherine Mansfield mused :

> I finished Stella Benson last night. I thought I might do her with Hope Mirrlees — two women, both protesting in the preface that their books are out of the ordinary. But no bridge could be thrown from one to the other. Miss Mirrlees lives in another world, and her world would *shudder* at Stella Benson. I don't.

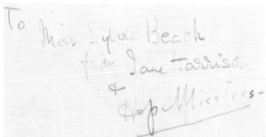

Portrait of Hope Mirrlees and Janes Harrison, Studio Landau, Paris (reduced), with detail of their inscription to Sylvia Beach. Courtesy of Princeton University Library.

On the contrary. They are two interesting problems, very intriguing. I hope I manage to say what I want to say.[70]

This last she does not manage, quite. But it is clear that Mansfield (and she would not have been alone) considered the novel worthy of serious intellectual engagement.

In 1922, following a disastrous love affair with "a man of singular beauty and fascination,"[71] Harrison destroyed her letters and other papers in a bonfire that Jane's friends subsequently (whether with or without justification cannot be determined) blamed on Hope's influence, and left Newnham and Cambridge forever. She and Mirrlees moved to Paris, where they wound up sharing rooms at the American Women's University Club, at 4 rue de Chevreuse. Sharing rooms was a significant economy for Harrison, whose income consisted of a bequest from her mother of three hundred pounds per year and a pension from Newnham of no more than fifty pounds annually. Annabel Robinson records the transition thusly :

> Before settling in Paris, Harrison and Mirrlees went for a little tour in Burgundy, and then to Nancy, to attend lectures by Emile Coue (perhaps Mirrlees's idea). [. . .] They then found accommodation at the Hotel de Londres, on the Rue Bonaparte, an "exquisite clean sardine-box" that was "most unsatisfactory" according to Mirrlees. Their rooms were on the fourth floor ; there was no sitting-room and no dining-room, and they were reduced to "seeking our omelettes, like Lear, in the storm." There was the added problem of uncertainty whether they could stay on there permanently, as the proprietor preferred temporary guests. For a while it looked as if they would have to return to England ; "space to move

and an occasional wash are all that I ask for."

They were rescued in November by Alys Russell, who obtained accommodation for them at the American University Women's Club, where they found themselves in "veritable clover", the best bedrooms, room-service breakfast, unlimited hot baths and admirable cooking "of the best French kind (touched by American) and more than that a personal care and kindness that goes to one's heart". Included with all this they were given at no extra cost a beautiful large sitting-room, "where I can breathe and work and even think, if the delights of Paris would leave me a free moment". For all this they paid the equivalent of 6/8d. a day. One wonders if Alys Russell in fact paid the extra cost of the sitting-room."[72]

Robinson, like most Harrison partisans, has a distinct animus toward Mirrlees.[73] Equally if not more likely is the possibility that Hope, who could certainly afford it, picked up the added expense herself. Similarly, the only reason it should be Mirrlees' idea to attend the lectures by Emile Coue, best remembered today for his formula for self-improvement by autosuggestion, "Day by day, in every way, I am getting better and better," is to relieve Harrison of the onus of bad taste. Both insinuations may be true. But they are insinuations and nothing more.

The very next year, Virginia Woolf came to Paris and, while there, visited Hope and Jane. Of the latter, whose ghost she would later place in *A Room Of One's Own*, she wrote :

This gallant old lady, very white, hoary, and sublime in a lace mantilla, took my fancy greatly ; partly for her superb high thinking agnostic ways, partly for her appearance. 'Alas,' she said, 'you and your sister and perhaps Lytton Strachey are the only ones of the younger generation I can respect. You alone carry on the traditions of our day.' This referred to the miserable defection of Fredegond [Shove] (mass ; confession ; absolution, and the rest of it.) 'There are thousands of Darwins' I said, to cheer her up. 'Thousands of Darwins !' she shrieked, clasping her mittened hands, and raising her eyes to Heaven. 'The Darwins are the blackest traitors of them all ! With that name !' she cried, 'that inheritance ! That magnificent record in the past !'

'Surely,' I cried, 'our Gwen is secure ?' 'Our Gwen,' she replied, 'goes to Church, (if not mass, still Church) every Sunday of her life. Her marriage, of course, may have weakened her brain. Jacques is, unfortunately, French. A wave of Catholicism has invaded the young Frenchmen. Their children are baptised ; their —' Here I stopped her. 'Good God,' I said, 'I will never speak to them again ! What's more, I've just written a flippant, frivolous, atheistic letter to that very household, which will arrive presently as the Host is elevated ; they'll spit me from their lips, spurn me in their hearts — and, in short, religion has accomplished one more of her miracles, and destroyed a friendship which I'm sure began in our mother's wombs !' All this eloquence left me dejected as a shovelful of cinders. Next week arrived your letter, which was the greatest relief in the world. Gwen is a militant atheist : the world renews itself : there is solid ground beneath my feet. I at once sent word to dear old Jane, who replied, a little inconsistently, 'Thank God.'[74]

This is a marvelous anecdote, and it seems a pity to cast cold water on it. But it makes no sense that one of the Cambridge Ritualists would speak so scornfully of baptism, confession, the Mass — in brief, of ritual itself.[75] Woolf must surely have misunderstood what Harrison said and in the seclusion of memory reconstructed it into something more entertaining than it actually was. She was always a more reliable source of fiction than of fact.

It is clear from the diaries, though, that when they met, Hope and Virginia talked about ideas. One entry mentions the three women discussing death until a University lady also present flushed and fled. In a longish letter dated January 6, 1923, Virginia wrote about her worries about her latest novel, thanked Hope for her praise of it, expressed interest in her next book, urged her to write a play for Hogarth Press, and ended with a lamentation of Hope's declaration in the Charing Cross Road, "Oh, but I can't write letters — shouldn't dream of it."[76]

Meanwhile, Jane and Hope enjoyed an intensely intellectual life.

24

Robinson describes their stay at Paul Desjardins' manor, a former Cistercian abbey at Pontigny, Burgundy, where invited intellectuals gathered for *"décades"* — ten-day structured explorations of assigned themes — as follows :

> Harrison loved the way the *entretiens* [colloquia] were run, with the mornings free to read and write. She loved the combination of freedom and discipline, the courtesy, and, be it said, the attention that was paid to her. She found herself admiring Desjardins for his intellectual strength, and Charles du Bos, who chaired the discussions, for the beautiful way he spoke French. [. . .] And then there was the stimulus of the other eminent participants, the 'magic' of their personalities. A group photo of this session includes (along with Paul Desjardins and Charles du Bos), Leon Shestov, Edith Wharton, André Maurois, Roger Martin du Gard, Jean Schlumberger and André Gide.

> In the midst of all this intellectual ferment Hope Mirrlees apparently staggered the French by remarking, 'Moi je n'ai pas de vie intérieure ! ('Myself, I have no interior life !') Perhaps she intended to shock, just as the Newnham students had in their debate on a woman's place, but it is conceivable that she meant it.[77]

At home in Paris, Jane and Hope entertained not only the Pontigny set and their Parisian and English friends, but also a growing number of Russian émigrés, including Marina Tsvetaeva, Alexei and Seraphima Remizov, philosopher Lev Shestov — and, foremost of all, Prince Dmitry Petrovich Sviatopolk Mirsky.

Prince Mirsky was an internationally famous man of letters, best known as the author of the two-volume *History of Russian Literature* (written, ironically enough, in English), a book which has remained in print since its first publication in 1926. In a letter to her friend Gilbert Murray after her second summer in Pontigny, Harrison wrote, "I have lost my aged heart to a Bear Prince — why did I not meet him 50 years ago, when I cld have clamoured to be his Princess [. . .]"[78] He in turn admired Harrison greatly and, according to Catriona Kelly, said that *Lud-in-the-Mist* "was the only recent English novel he'd read that he actually liked."[79] In his biography of Mirsky, Gerald Stanton Smith writes that in 1926 when Mirsky was looking for funding to start up the Russian-language literary journal *Vyorsts*, "He went first to Jane Harrison, who immediately stumped up £50 of the £200 Mirsky reckoned he needed, and recommended several other useful contacts."[80] (In light of Jane's financial situation, this was a puzzlingly great deal of money, as Mirsky himself wrote in a letter to Remizov : "Though I don't know how she came up with it. She herself has none."[81]) In the third and final issue of *Vyorsts*, he reviewed Mirrlees' novels.

This exposure to the Russian literary-establishment-in-exile was to result directly in two books of translations by Harrison and Mirrlees — *The Book of the Bear*, and *Life of the Arch-Priest Avvakum by Himself*. The indirect influence of their works on *Lud-in-the-Mist*, however, would ultimately be more significant.

In 1924, Mirrlees' second novel, *The Counterplot*, was published by Collins. To a reader today, it is even more daunting than was *Madeleine*. In a classic overreaction to the didacticism of her first novel, she chose this time to explain *nothing*. Characters come and go without identification, expressing opinions upon matters and people about which and whom the reader knows nothing. It is like being trapped without a friend in somebody else's family reunion. Yet though it is much more difficult to follow and understand than the first novel, it is also infinitely more bearable. Hope's current avatar, Teresa, is moody, self-centered, and judgmental, but nowhere near the hideous prig Madeleine was. There is a sense that the author almost likes her.

The plot is simple. An emotionally cool young woman of literary temperament with a pleasant-yet-despised suitor, finds herself the object of romantic attention from a young seminarian. Though she does not respond to his advances, she offhandedly decides to write a play as an entertainment for the family. "The Key" — one hundred pages long, and included in its entirety — reveals Teresa's subconscious desires, and her hidden passion for the young priest-to-be.

This play-within-a-novel is also a *roman à clef*, again utilizing all of Hope's family as characters. That these characters are radically unlike their counterparts in the rest of the novel reveals Mirrlees' source strategy. Her family was utilized as a repertory company, available to play whatever roles were needed, so that one might be here the hero and there the villain, yet everywhere identifiably himself. Nor did this go unnoticed. The granddaughter of Alexander Moncrieff, Lina's youngest sibling, reports that family were horrified by the novel "because of assumed autobiographical elements, and there was a quotation that did the rounds (I don't know whether authentic or not) describing the heroine's sister as 'a cat in perpetual season', which was a central part of the corpus delicti."[82]

The plot, involving a virtuous nun who is seduced by a dashing villain who in his turn falls in love with her, a less-than-virtuous nun who betrays her, and a wicked old witch-woman causing trouble behind the scenes, is all rather predictable and conventional hugger-mugger. (In 1923, Woolf requested a play from Mirrlees for Hogarth Press[83]; if this is it, then it's probably a good thing that Mirrlees apparently never submitted it.) But Teresa's family is baffled by the play anyway, though once presented its implications are clear enough to both Teresa and her intended.

The theme of the novel, again, is the conflict between life and art. Again, they cannot be resolved, as, ironically, the seminarian is driven back into the arms of the Church by Teresa's admission of desire. This time, though, rather than going mad, the heroine simply has a quiet moment of insight into herself and into the nature of the world.

"My gifted friend Hope Mirrlees has written a wonderful novel, *Counterplot*, in which she shows that only in and through the pattern of art, or it may be of religion, which is a form of art, do we at all seize and understand the tangle of experience which we call Life,"[84] Jane Harrison wrote, neatly epitomizing the novel's intentions. In 1955, thirty years after he first read it, Christopher Isherwood obtained, after long advertisement, a copy of *The Counterplot*, which he then reread. He wrote in his diary :

> I find I know whole passages of it nearly by heart. It must have been one of the truly 'formative' books in my life. And yet it represents so much that I used to imagine I hated and was fighting to the death — Cambridge cleverness and the whole *Waste Land* technique of describing moods by quotations from the classics — in fact, indulging in moods that were nothing else but the quotations themselves. It's a second-rate book, but I still feel some of the charm it used to have for me. And just because its 'sophistication' is transparently naïve, I find it warmer and more sympathetic than that of the early Aldous Huxley.[85]

Which is a fair representation of the book from an unlikely source. The novel has, alas, not aged well, though it was warmly received, translated into French, and sold briskly enough that a second edition was arranged two years later.

Scattered within the books are remarks that cast an interesting light on Mirrlees' writing. At one point, the protagonist (freely altering Shakespeare's lines) muses,

> . . . but fancy was nothing —
> Tell me where is Fancy bred ?
> *Not* in the heart
> *Nor* in the head

nearly all young Englishmen had fancy — a fancy fed by *Alice in Wonderland*, and the goblin arabesques on the cover of *Punch* ; a certain romantic historical sense too that thrills to *Puck of Pook's Hill* and the *Three Musketeers* — oh yes, and, unlike Frenchmen, they probably all cherish a hope that never quite dies of one day playing Anthony to some astonishingly provocative lady — foreign probably, passionate and sophisticated as the heroine of *Three Weeks*, mysterious as Rider Haggard's *She*. But all that is just part of the average English outfit — national, ubiquitous, undistinguished, like a sense of humour and the proverbial love of fair play.[86]

This is a startling rant to hear coming from the mouth of a fantasist, as well as being possibly the first feminist critique of the sexist masculine roots of genre fantasy. Nor is it an aberration, for the same theme pops up again later, when the heroine is attending her sister's wedding in a thinly-disguised Bicester House.[87] When one guest comments, "Well, one couldn't have a more Christmassy house. It always seems to me like the house one suddenly comes upon in a wood in a fairy story. One expects the door to be opened by a badger in livery," the protagonist thinks in fury :

> Again that bastard Fancy ! The same sort of thing had occurred
> to her herself — when she was a child ; but the imagination of
> a man ought to be different from the fancy of a child.[88]

To understand this, it helps to realize that, at the time, adult fantasy as we understand it today was practically nonexistent, and that most of what *did* exist was presented with a wink and a smirk. Victorian fairy-mania had left its stain. Fantasy had not yet worked its way entirely free of the nursery, and wouldn't without the help of writers like Mirrlees who had neither patience nor nostalgia for discarded childish things.

Here she is, raging against common people and the everyday world :

> Yes ; their minds were sterile, frivolous . . . *un-Platonic* — that
> was the word for expressing the lack she felt in that crew ; un-
> Platonic, *because they could not make myths.* For them the shoemak-
> er at his last, the potter at his wheel, the fishwives of the mar-
> ket-place, new-born babies and dead men, never suddenly grew
> transparent, allowing to glimmer through them the contours of
> a stranger world. For them Dionysus, whirling in his frantic
> dance, never suddenly froze into the still cold marble of
> Apollo.[89]

Yet here at the end, when Teresa has realized the depth of her own folly, the song turns around upon itself :

> Oh, foolish race of myth-makers ! Starving, though the
> plain is golden with wheat ; though their tent is pitched between

two rivers, dying of thirst ; calling for the sun when it is dark, and for the moon when it is midday.[90]

Both plaints are equally heartfelt : her yearning for something beyond the quotidian and her scornful awareness that she was yearning for something that did not exist.

A less ambitious book would have served her better. As it stands, her protagonist moons through the houses and lives of the wealthy and aristocratic that Mirrlees knew so well, drifting past the sewing room, resolutely focused on her own elevated thoughts, without showing us what the sewing room looked like or what the servants were doing in it. At times the reader wants to shove her aside and gawk. It's a genuine pity. Had Mirrlees written it as a novel of manners, *The Counterplot* might well be still read today. As her nephew mused, reflecting on childhood days in "Christmassy" Bicester House, "This was a sort of jolly old kind of world, which does not really exist any more."[91]

In retrospect, however, Hope was making progress. And it was in this same year that she and Jane began a sporadic correspondence with a writer who was to have a profound influence on her fiction.

The early nineteen-twenties were a hothouse time for early modern fantasy. E.R. Eddison's *The Worm Ouroboros* appeared in 1922. Lord Dunsany's *The King of Elfland's Daughter*, with its treatment of Faerie and our own world as distinct and equal realms, appeared in 1924. James Branch Cabell's *Jurgen* was published in 1919 in the United States and in 1921, revised, in England. David Garnett's *Lady into Fox* came out in 1922, James Stephens' *Deirdre* in 1923, and Norman Douglas' *They Went* in 1920. It may even be significant that Hugh Lofting's *The Story of Doctor Dolittle*, set largely in Puddleby-on-the-Marsh was published in 1920. Going a bit further afield, Gerald

Bullett's 1924 novel, *Mr. Godly Beside Himself* featured a world-weary businessman who enters Faerie, and was an eloquent plea for the reconciliation of reason and imagination. Even David Lindsay's *A Voyage to Arcturus* (1920) has to be taken into account, given its acknowledged influence on both Tolkien and C. S. Lewis.[92]

There is no record of Hope Mirrlees reading any of these works.[93] (Though given that Garnett was a friend and a founding director of Nonesuch Press, and that his wife Ray, who was the original of the protagonist of *Lady into Fox*, provided the illustrations for *The Book of the Bear*, it's a good bet that she read at least one.) Certainly she would have loathed many of them. But one does not have to approve of a work to be influenced by it. Indeed, some of the most influential works are those an author argues against. In her typically high-handed fashion, however, Mirrlees publicly acknowledged only one fantastic writer, and that one a man who is today, among English-speaking readers, even more obscure than she is.

Alexei Remizov, novelist, short-story writer, and painter, was a Russian émigré who had been living in Paris since 1921. He is a significant figure in Russian literature, though largely as a pioneer and influence on other writers, and one fitting neatly in the stream of influence that leads from the Archpriest Avvakum (whose autobiography Jane and Hope translated) to Vladimir Nabokov. When, in 1926, Harrison and Mirrlees published a small collection of bear tales, translated from Russian, his two pieces were the only contributions from a living author.

It was Remizov who made obvious to Mirrlees the literary possibilities inherent in fairy-tales and folklore. She, in turn, wrote a study of him entitled "Quelques aspects de l'art d'Alexis Mikhailovich Remizov" which appeared in the January 15 - March 15, 1926 Arts and Philosophy issue of *Le Journal de Psychologie Normale et Pathologique*.[94]

A careful study of this essay reveals almost as much about Mirrlees as it does about Remizov. In it, she cited two living critics, one living painter (Monet, however, died that same year), and twenty-nine writers, all but one of whom were dead,[95] the majority of them since before she was born. She may have hobnobbed with Virginia Woolf, T.S. Eliot, and Gertrude Stein, but William Morris, Sir Walter Scott, and Walter Savage Landor were more to her conservative taste.

Remizov, according to Mirrlees, had the capacity for physical identification, and could thus express the tragedy of life in a comic fashion. He was sometimes ecstatic, but never sentimental. His writing was Russian in a way that Tolstoy's and Dostoevski's were not, but Pushkin's and Gogol's were. It was spiritual. It contained aphorisms and pretty observations. His overflowing pages were filled with a richness of detail and of vocabulary. Above all, she praised him as a humorist.

Whatever small good her article did him, Remizov more than repaid through example. It is striking how well the above praises describe Mirrlees' third book, *Lud-in-the-Mist*, though not her first two novels. While she cannot by any stretch be described as "Russian," the gentle and lovingly-described countryside of Dorimare is transparently that of her native England, perhaps brought to her attention by the success of Remizov's treatment of his own homeland. Humor in particular was starkly missing from *Madeleine* and *The Counterplot*, novels written before Remizov showed her how closely interrelated humor was to tragedy, and how the bright colors of the one brought out the darkness of the other.

Most importantly, Remizov demonstrated to Mirrlees the potential power of folklore. In so doing, he freed her from the strictures of realism, and pointed her toward a mode of writing — fantasy — in which her obsessive theme could finally find resolution. In an introduction co-written with Harrison to *The Book of the Bear*, Mirrlees (it seems likeliest) wrote :

But Remizov is a far more cunning craftsman than Aesop, and when he chooses can do the most difficult thing in the world — write fables that have no moral.

Perhaps he learned the secret from the main source of his inspiration — folk tales. Just as Mussorsky and Rimsky-Korsakov wove their modern music round folk-melodies, so Remizov has evolved his elaborate style and intensely individual fantasy from the simple rhythms of Russian folk-tales, and the foolish doings of their heroes. [. . .] A genuine folk-tale is like a dream . . . a real dream, not a made-up one.[96]

The Book of the Bear was published in 1926 — the same year as

Lud-in-the-Mist and her essay. Mirrlees would have been translating folktales, analyzing Remizov, and working on her novel all at the same time.

In April, 1925, Woolf wrote to a friend describing Paris as "a hostile brilliant alien city. Nancy Cunard and Hope Mirrlees and myriads of ineffective English live here, or rather hop from rock to rock."[97] Hope and Jane apparently agreed, for after Harrison's two-year term of residency at the American Club ended that spring, they left. For a time they wandered "far flown in the midi" (dropping in on, among other people, André Gide), in a vacation Harrison found "peaceful and pleasant after three strenuous years in Paris."[98] They then returned to London, where Hope found a "tiny mousetrap of a house" at 11 Mecklenburgh Street (since destroyed in the Blitz) on the edge of Bloomsbury, convenient to the Nonesuch Press, which was engaged in publishing *The Book of the Bear*.[99] They settled down to learning Icelandic, so they could read the Eddas.

That same year, Woolf wrote to a correspondent, "do you admire her novels — I can't get an ounce of joy from them."[100] So it's unlikely she ever read Mirrlees' masterpiece, *Lud-in-the-Mist*, published by Collins in 1926. What would she have made of it ? Would she even have understood it ? Surely the author of *Orlando* (which includes Hope Mirrlees in its rather lengthy list of acknowledgments) would have appreciated, at least, the radical freedoms of narrative the novel takes. Alas, we shall never know

Lud-in-the-Mist is dedicated "To the Memory of My Father." William Julius Mirrlees died suddenly in Buenos Aires on January 28, 1923. Given that Mirrlees' second book was published in 1924, it is reasonable to suppose that her third was begun in the wake of his death. The foolish, prosperous merchant protagonist, Nathaniel Chanticleer, with his self-satisfaction and his unsuccessful marriage,[101] is transparently Hope's father, again taken from Hope's repertory company of characters. Yet now he has been forgiven for whatever sin caused him to be so harshly portrayed in her first two novels. Now he is the protagonist and, for the first time in Hope's writings, the protagonist grows and rises above himself to become the book's hero.

Also recognizable among the characters are Hope's mother as Chanticleer's wife, Dame Marigold ; her sister as their daughter Prunella[102] ; and her aunt as Nat's old foolish-wise nurse, Hempie. Noticeably missing from the playbill — and wisely so — is Mirrlees herself.

The novel takes its name from the city of Lud-in-the-Mist (a play on the flower love-in-the-mist, a perennial popular in sixteenth-century gardens)[103] and begins :

> The free state of Dorimare was a very small country, but, seeing that it was bounded on the south by the sea and on the north and east by mountains, while its centre consisted of a rich plain, watered by two rivers, a considerable variety of scenery and vegetation was to be found within its borders. Indeed, towards the west, in striking contrast with the pastoral sobriety of the central plain, the aspect of the country became, if not tropical, at any rate distinctly exotic. Nor was this to be wondered at, perhaps ; for beyond the Debatable Hills (the boundary of Dorimare in the west) lay Fairyland. There had, however been no intercourse between the two countries for many centuries.[104]

So complete is the rupture between the two countries that the name of the latter is never spoken in Dorimare, and the vilest name a man can be called is Son of a Fairy. The vilest crime, moreover, that can be committed is to eat fairy fruit. Yet fairy fruit can always be found by those who desire it, and at the time the novel opens it is being smuggled into Lud-in-the-Mist, and fed to the town's children. Its effects — madness, suicide, death — are not at all pleasant.

It is up to the Mayor and High Seneschel of Lud-in-the-Mist — none other than Chanticleer himself — to put an end to the smuggling. But he and the other Magistrates are half-asleep and out of touch with the doings of the common folk. Moreover, Chanticleer's is an uneasy sleep, and he is afraid of what he might wake into. He likes to wander the Fields of Grammary, where Lud's citizens are buried and memorialized, contemplating the dead and envying their lot. And he is opposed by the loathsome doctor Endymion Leer, who slyly and ironically sets about poisoning the hearts of the town against him.

Further complicating matters is the fact that before the revolution that established a mercantile republic in Dorimare the country had strong affinities with Fairyland. Its then-ruler, the cruel, hunchbacked, and beautiful Duke Aubrey is still revered by the common folk.

Dorimare is, in fact, quite a neat model for Mirrlees' family background : dull, respectable, and prosperous on the surface, but with an aristocratic and romantic past, delicately laced with scandal.[105]

Neil Gaiman, in his introduction to the Millennium "Fantasy Masterworks" edition of *Lud-in-the-Mist*, deftly summed up Mirrlees' magisterial command of form in this work : "The book begins as a travelogue or a history, becomes a pastorale, a low comedy, a high comedy, a ghost story and a detective story." And yet these are not separate sections crudely cobbled together, but interwoven strands of a single sinuous narrative written by a woman in complete control of her matter. As Gaiman concluded, "The writing is elegant, supple, effective and haunting : the author demands a great deal from her readers, which she repays many times over."[102] This last cries out for a specific example. A pleached alley is one in which tree branches have been interlaced or entwined to form a sort of arbor or tunnel. Here is how Mirrlees describes one :

> To the imaginative, it is always something of an adventure to walk down a pleached alley. You enter boldly enough, but very soon you find yourself wishing you had stayed outside — it is not air that you are breathing, but silence, the almost palpable silence of trees. And is the only exit that small round hole in

the distance ? Why, you will never be able to squeeze through that ! You must turn back . . . too late ! The spacious portal by which you entered has in its turn shrunk to a small round hole.[107]

This is a kind of conjuring-trick. It is also distinctly out of step with its era. At a time when Virginia Woolf and Ernest Hemingway and Gertrude Stein and however many others were discarding such nine-teenth-century vermiculation as the second person rhetorical, italics, exclamation marks, literary hyperventilating, and auctorial dictation of emotion, in relentless pursuit of a leaner, more aerodynamic style, Hope Mirrlees determinedly clutched her embroidered prose all the more closely to herself. "It is best to let sleeping facts lie," she aphorized, and "He who rides the wind needs must go where his steed carries him," and "Reason is only a drug, and its effects cannot be permanent." She strewed the work with archaic words, obsolete diction, antiquarian objects. She created rather hobbitish names for her characters (Florian Baldbreeches, Ebeneezor Prim, Diggory Carp, Penstemmon Fliperarde, Ambrosine Pyepowders, to mention but five) and impossibly romantic settings for them (Moongrass, Mothgreen, the Elfin Marches, Swan-on-the-Dapple). It is a dissident work, written in full awareness of what the proper literary writers were up to, and in its refusal to go along with them daringly defiant.

Not that anybody noticed, of course. But it was brave nonetheless.

The climax of the novel occurs when Nathaniel Chanticleer, the most unheroic of heroes, goes into the land from which no one returns, where the sun and moon do not shine, birds are dreams, stars are visions, and immortal flowers grow — in short, the Celtic land of the dead — to rescue his son (and, rather incidentally, his daughter Prunella and her classmates) from the market of souls. His weapon is the Law, for Fairyland is delusion and Law, occupying the same psychic space with its legal fictions and pervasive yet intangible presence, is the homoeopathic antidote to delusion.

But Law, reason, and common sense can only take Chanticleer so far. There, at the edge of the knowable, he takes one further step, into the abyss. This bold act — by protagonist and author alike — unexpectedly reveals the novel to be, like *Paris*, a re-enactment of the Eleusinian mysteries. Chanticleer thus becomes an initiate, qualified to handle the instruments of Mystery — life and death.

It has to be acknowledged that here, at the very heart of the novel, there is a strange emptiness or silence. Chanticleer takes a step into the darkness at the end of one chapter, and then the next chapter begins after he has returned from it. This inspired Joanna Russ to write "The Zanzibar Cat," a story which is both an extremely graceful pastiche of *Lud-in-the-Mist* and a razor-toothed parody of it. As Russ herself explained :

> I had read the novel and found the end unsatisfying. The author had bonked right into the wall that many fantasists bark their shins on. After practically promising us yes, you will be able to see faery for yourself, faery is all-important the source of the story &c. when it comes right down to it you (or rather she) can't paint a picture of it. Like C. S. Lewis's *Narnia* stories, the transitions into the Other World are lovely but once you're there, what are you going to do ? What is there ?[108]

The novel resolves all at its end, though on a pleasantly ambiguous note. The two lands are reconciled. The apple trees cross the stone wall to eat pine cones on the other side, and *Lud-in-the-Mist* throws wide its gates to receive its destiny. Chanticleer is lauded as a hero — a role he finds uncomfortable — but though his marriage is healed, he is not. While he is incontestably a better man than he was at the beginning of the novel, he remains a melancholy one, still not truly at home in his world.

But what does it all *mean* ?

The original source of Mirrlees' key image, the fairy fruit, must assuredly have been Christina Rossetti's "Goblin Market," with the fairy fruit that, once tasted, leave one yearning forever for more — which, however, is forever denied the sufferer, for a second taste cures the effects of the first. Yet Rossetti's ostensible message (for she vehemently denied the sexual subtext that seems so obvious to the modern reader) is worlds apart from Mirrlees'. For where Rossetti's work ends with the repentant sister first warning her children to steer clear of fairy fruit and then homilizing :

For there is no friend like a sister,
In calm or stormy weather,
To cheer one on the tedious way,
To fetch one if one goes astray,
To lift one if one totters down,
To strengthen whilst one stands.

(a sentiment wholly alien to Hope's philosophy and family history alike), Mirrlees' characters come to accept the necessity of the fairy fruit and, indeed, end up shipping it in candied form to all the nations of the world. She has kept the outward shape of Rossetti's conceit but transformed its essence.

Gaiman, in his Millennium introduction, grumbled at seeing a Marxist interpretation of *Lud*, and as recently as April 5, 2001, the normally insightful Mary Beard wrote in the *TLS* that the novel ultimately comes to involve "fundamental questions of how a society and its members understand their own history, and how they make sense of the conflicts embedded in social class and political power." Yet Mirrlees' political message, taken seriously, boils down to the admonition that the gentry must be attentive to the needs of the rabble. Such misreadings only demonstrate how radically different the artistic agenda of the fantasist is from that of a "mainstream"[109] writer.

"A little of the measure of the greatness of a writer is precisely the difference between the things which he says and of the things that he knows,"[110] Mirrlees once wrote. So perhaps, in a sense, she brought this confusion upon herself. Yet her intents are not all that hard to discern. She herself spelled them out in the book's opening epigram, taken from Jane Harrison :

The Sirens stand, as it would seem, to the ancient and the modern, for the impulses in life as yet immoralised, imperious longings, ecstasies, whether of love or art, or philosophy, magical voices calling to a man from his "Land of Heart's Desire," and to which if he hearken it may be that he will return no more — voices, too, which, whether a man sail by or stay to hearken, still sing on.

There, right at the outset, is the explanation of what *Lud-in-the-Mist* is actually about. It is about immoralised impulses, imperious longings, ecstasies of love or art or philosophy, magical voices. Since these voices speak in many languages, each to the private heart of the auditor, it is small wonder that they cannot be easily synopsized or epitomized. Small wonder, too, that the novel holds such great power over so many of its readers.

The reviews were, with few exceptions, strongly positive.

This was the high-water mark of her career.

Harrison had returned to London weary and possibly already ill. "In the summer of 1927," according to Robinson, "she experienced some kind of attack and suffered 'many strange and terrible things'."[111]   Hope was, of course, protective. Victoria de Bunsen, another of Harrison's former Newnham students, wrote to Jessie Stewart of a visit to see Jane :

My dearest Jessie

I have just been to JEH. Hope was of course *most* ungracious & very overwrought I thought. She said it was out of the question for anyone to see her, it wd. kill her. There was a nice nurse but she had terribly missed her nurse cousin Miss Lane who left on 4 just before she was so desperately ill. . . . I *left*. Then Hope went up to Jane who said she must see me, so H. had to run after me into the street. I went up for one moment. She is in the tiny back drawing room. She doesn't look washed — & very thin, just a [illegible] passive. She said, '*All* the life's gone out of me,' her voice fairly strong. Hope reads to her & the last 2 days she's better, temp. down each morn [?] a better night. I gave her all yr messages, love & sympathy. She looked so pleased. It is difficult. Obviously Hope *wishes* to keep everybody away — & said she would not write to Jane's friends or even answer the phone ! but the man servant 'could do it !' Yet she is *very* anxious & very devoted. They have a very nice lady doctor now & *close* by. H. said her nieces call. I wonder who else of her friends are looking after her ? I shall every other day or so — & I will let you know & will *go* again before long. . . . They say sort of pneumonia, lung and heart, & phlebitis.[112]

At this time of great personal pressure, Mirrlees began to sabotage her own career. On June 28, 1927, she wrote to Lady Ottoline Morrell :

It was also frightfully kind of you to pave the way for my publishing that thing (it so pleased me you liked it so much) in the Criterion. At first I was so excited, but on re-reading it I see that I simply couldn't expect Eliot (apart from the fact that he would probably think it very silly & bad) as an Anglo-Catholic to accept it. After all, it plays, as if they were only coloured balls, with conceptions which to him must be the most solemn of spiritual realities — &, really, he couldn't be expected to print it. But it was so dear of you to bother.[113]

The illness had its ups and downs. On January 17, 1928, Harrison had recovered enough to attend Thomas Hardy's funeral in Westminster Abbey as one of the dignitaries. Whether Mirrlees accompanied her is not recorded, though given the elderly lady's condition it seems likely.

Two months later, on April 15, 1928, Jane Ellen Harrison died of leukemia. Two days after that, Woolf recorded in her diary :

Before that, crossing the graveyard in the bitter windy rain, we saw Hope and a dark cultivated woman. But on they went past us, with the waver of an eye. Next moment I heard "Virginia" and turned and there was Hope coming back — "Jane died yesterday," she murmured, half asleep, talking distraught, "out of herself." We kissed by Cromwell's daughter's grave, where Shelley used to walk, for Jane's death. She lay dead outside the graveyard in that back room where we saw her lately raised on her pillows, like a very old person whom life has tossed up and left : exalted, satisfied, exhausted. Hope the colour of dirty brown paper. Then to the office, then home to work here ; and now to work and work, as hard as I can.[114]

It was Oliver Cromwell's grand-daughter who was buried in St. George's Fields, behind the Foundling Hospital and adjacent to the Mecklenburgh flat. But despite her typically casual way with facts, Woolf saw through to the human moment. When her husband Leonard wrote a rather stiff and formal condolence note, Virginia added a postscript saying, "Anyhow, what a comfort for you to have been all you were to her."[115]

Nearly four decades later, Hope still remembered, not the exact words, but the gist of that postscript. In a letter to Valerie Eliot, consoling her on the death of her husband, she wrote, "It was only one line but it was more comforting than all the other letters put together : 'But remember what you have had.' "[116]

Harrison was buried in St. Marylebone Cemetery, Finchley, North London. Woolf attended the funeral and was not impressed. "Very drab," she sniffed, and "it was only barely full of the dingiest people."[117]

This was the death, as well, of Mirrlees' literary ambitions.

Mirrlees was in her early forties when Harrison died. She had a thriving literary career, a supportive editor and agent, good contacts, and an independent income. (Members of Hope's family, her brother in particular, were convinced that the Bloomsbury crowd were all after Mirrlees' money. There is nothing to indicate that any of them benefited financially from her friendship, however.) If Virginia Woolf's magisterial essay, *A Room of One's Own*, is to be taken literally, she had everything a woman required to make it as a writer.

She was also at the peak of her productivity, turning out essays and articles for the *Athenaeum*, the *Times*, and even a French journal of psychology.[118] So successful was she that the May 1926 issue of the British edition of *Vogue* included her in their regular feature, "We Nominate for the Hall of Fame" :

Miss Hope Mirrlees : Because she is the authoress of "The Counterplot", the most brilliant novel that has appeared for the past eighteen months : because her volume, "Paris", the only good dada poem in English, was the admiration of Monsieur André Gide : and because her erudition is equaled only by her wit.

As further evidence of the energy and ambition Mirrlees displayed at her peak, consider a recent literary excavation from the *Christian Science Monitor* :

Eighty years ago next week, on July 24, 1926, a dinner party in England took an unusual turn. Helen Hope Mirrlees, a feminist poet and author, posed an intriguing question : What will marriage be like in 100 years ?

The dozen or so assembled guests, described as "famous men and women of the cultured upper classes," rose to the challenge, offering a range of domestic scenarios for 2026.

Ms. Mirrlees herself speculated that in the next century, men and women might reverse roles. As recounted in *The Times* of London, she asked, "Will it become an accepted thing that men, when it suits their temperament, take up the job of housekeeper and allow their more pushful better halves to go out and earn the family livelihood ?"[119]

The ensuing conversation was lively and occasionally prescient. What's notable about it, however, is that with a working writer's fine sense of economy and genteel self-promotion, Mirrlees promptly placed it in a paying market.

But in late February of 1928, about a month and a half before Harrison's death, at a time when it must have been obvious that death was imminent, Mirrlees called Collins and peremptorily demanded to be released from a contract for her next novel. A little unhappily, Sir Godfrey

Collins agreed. Hope's agent returned her the canceled document, adding, "As soon as your new novel is ready, I hope to have the pleasure of seeing you again, so that we may arrange where I am to offer it first."[120]

And that was that. No trace of that fourth novel has ever been found. Even its title, if it was ever begun, is not known.

Had Mirrlees been a working writer, the necessity of keeping a roof over her head would have forced her to keep at her typewriter. But she was cursed with wealth. Faced with adversity, she had the means simply to give up.

Besides, Hope had found a new enthusiasm. She began to gather materials for a life of Jane Ellen Harrison.

Mary Beard recounts the long and faintly ridiculous history of the biography and of the Harrison Archive in *The Invention of Jane Harrison*. The biography began as a supposed collaboration between Hope and Jessie Stewart, who had been Harrison's prize student some years before her. Thirty years ensued of endless back-and-forthing, recriminations and stormy scenes, Hope's histrionic decision that she was too close to the subject to write objectively about her, and enormous difficulties finding a publisher interested in a book about a woman academic. Finally, in 1959, Jessie Stewart's solo biography, *Jane Ellen Harrison : A Portrait from Letters* was published at last. "Next, I thank Hope Mirrlees, Jane Harrison's latest and closest friend, who as her literary executor has given me *carte blanche* to select among her letters. She will, I hope, some day give us her own version of Jane's later years," Stewart wrote testily in the acknowledgments.

It was an innocent, rather bland little book. But it sent Hope into a frenzy of recrimination anyway. "But Oh Jessie how *could* you have put in some of the parts in the 'Francis & Frances' chapter ? . . . I am *horribly* distressed that this has been published. Jane would simply have *loathed* it."[121]

All this time, Hope was managing the Harrison Archive. Because Harrison had burned her papers upon leaving Newnham, there were almost no primary materials. Hope threw herself into the project anyway. Decades' worth of interviews, correspondence, judicious pruning and careful rephrasing of memories finally resulted in a body of papers dealing entirely with . . . itself.

43

It would all be comic, if it weren't for the destruction of a genuine literary talent. There were still books in the pipeline (*Life of the Arch-Priest Avvakum by Himself*, translated by Mirrlees and Harrison, with an introduction by their friend Prince Mirsky,[122] came out from the Hogarth Press in 1929, and *Le Choc en retour*, a translation of *The Counterplot*, appeared in France that same year) when Harrison died. But in the fifty years that followed, she published exactly one chapbook's worth of amateurish poetry and a single volume of biography.

Mirrlees had also undergone another transformation, greater than that of novelist to biographer. In 1976, a glowing chapbook introduction by Raymond Mortimer touched upon Mirrlees' friendship with Jane Harrison, and then added, somewhat surprisingly, "She has been profoundly influenced in her Catholicism by that great scholar, finding in Greek religion prototypes of Christian faith."[123]

Jansenism, the religious philosophy (condemned as heretical by papal bulls in 1653 and 1713) that played such a major role in Madeleine, was an obscure strain of Catholicism. Similarly, the play-within-a-novel in *The Counterplot* was subtitled *An Auto Sacramental*, an auto sacramental being a Spanish medieval drama dealing with the mystery of the Mass in allegory. *Paris* featured schoolgirl blasphemies from the rather innocent "Le petit Jésus fait pipi" to the faintly creepy description of life-size wax dolls, dressed as if for First Holy Communion, displayed in the windows of the large shops :

Waxen Pandoras in white veils and ties of her own decking ;
Catéchisme de Perseverance,
The decrees of the Seven Oecumenical Councils reduced to the *format*
of the *Bibliothèque Rose*,
Première Communion,
(Prometheus has swallowed the bait)
Petits Lycéens
Por-no-gra-phie,
Charming pigmy brides,
Little Saint Hugh avenged —

THE CHILDREN EAT THE JEW.[124]

From her earliest writings, Mirrlees had displayed a knowledgeable fascination with the Catholic Church odd in a woman who came from a family of Scottish Covenanters. Now, she was to take the final step. On November 30, 1929, Woolf cattily wrote, "It is said that Hope has become a Roman Catholic on the sly. Certainly she has grown very fat — too fat for a woman in middle age who uses her brains & so I suspect the rumour is true."[125]

If Woolf was correct, this was a sudden conversion. On May 19 of that same year, Mirrlees had written Lady Ottoline Morrell of a friend's futile attempts to win her over. "What antagonises you in the Vedas, in a lesser degree antagonises me in Catholicism — the cut & dried way of labelling various psychological phenomena as sinful. I can't acknowledge Sin. I so absolutely agree with Jane that there is only the Good & the Better, & to lose one's salvation is to choose the Good when one could take the Better. This condemnation of everything except a cold abstraction they call God that you object to in the Vedas seems to me the Catholic belief in Sin pushed to its logical conclusion."[126]

In *The Counterplot*, the heroine's mother (but not her father) is a Catholic, and heartbroken when her second daughter renounces the Faith in order to marry a man who can only inherit his ancestral house as a protestant. Perhaps this reflects some incident in Hope's family history. The great house is an identical twin for Bicester, which T.S. Eliot considered his favorite house in all the world, and which Hope's sister Margot moved into when she married Major Aubrey Coker, known informally as Bolo. Further, the Moncrieffs were old aristocracy, and the old families of Scotland went in and out of Catholicism frequently, as the political winds shifted.[127] To complicate matters, Catriona Kelly recalled that, "Also, again from my mother's reminiscences, Lina and her husband globe-trotted through different religions, and Lina ended up a Christian Scientist — my mother thought, because WJ had died when they were still in that phase and it struck her as disloyal to move on again."[128]

Contrarian as always, when Mirrlees embraced Catholicism, she did so with the zealousness of a true convert. Her sister-in-law, Frances Mirrlees, used to tease her with a limerick :

> A certain young lady called Hope
> Delighted in teasing the Pope.
> She said, "Just for fun

Could you make me a nun ?"
Said the Pope, "dear Hope, not a hope."[129]

In the 1970s, when *Paris* was reprinted for the first time ever in the short-lived *Virginia Woolf Quarterly*, Mirrlees carefully bowdlerized it, removing all the blasphemous bits.

In France, her nephew took her to wash her feet in a famous holy fountain with curative powers, and recalls her being thrilled by the experience. "Hopie had become a Catholic (perhaps converted by Monsignor Ronald Knox who was a celebrated priest at the time)," he wrote, "and because of her deeply and totally sincere Christian faith, was not in the least afraid of death. Good luck to her. I envied her."[130] She had found the reconciliation of workaday reality and transcendence she yearned for.

Anthony Powell characterized Hope Mirrlees in the 1940s as "unmarried, with Bloomsbury associations in early life, though now settled down to a less exacting intellectual condition of comfortable upper-middlebrowdom."[131] She did not entirely abandon the literary world. A biography of Lady Ottoline Morrell notes her being at a tea party also attended by William Butler Yeats, Dilys Powell, and Walter de la Mare. But she was now a presence rather than a potential power.

With Harrison gone, Hope took up an apartment with her mother at 1 Thurloe Close, opposite Brompton Oratory. The scattered mentions of Mirrlees in Woolf's letters and diaries no longer recorded her envious exasperation with the younger woman, but only the slow loss of Hope's looks, and her increasing dedication to her lapdog. On January 21, 1928, before Harrison's death, Woolf had written to Clive Bell, "Hope too well up in the Romantics for my taste ; but a woman of wit none the less, and passable, even now, in a darkish room."[132] By

November 30, 1929, this judgment had been downgraded to "She has sat herself down under the shade. It is strange to see beauty — she had something elegant & individual — go out, like a candle flame. Julian, for instance, could not see, I think, that Hope had ever been a young & attractive woman. She has some vigor of mind though."[133] In late 1930, she wrote of "a sticky valiant evening at Hope's"[134] and in 1932 noted "dinner with Hope last night : her stuffed black dachshund sausage stretched along my knee."[135] In 1933, she jotted, ". . . in comes Hope : lost her neck ; grown stubby waxy but affable. . . . The black dachshund on Hope's knee. Has a snappy screech."[136] In 1934 she invited Mirrlees to visit, adding, "And bring Marie, I mean the dachshund, to introduce a human note."[137] After which she concluded in her diary, "Not a very good evening. Talk scattered & surface patterning. Hope & her dog distracting."[138] In 1935, she wrote, "A very nice party at MacCarthy's last night . . . Hope on a diet of course."[139]

It is a dreary recital. The malice that enlivened Woolf's earlier passages was replaced by a tolerant and understated pity. She no longer bothered to comment on Mirrlees' literary opinions at all.

There is a photograph in Lyndall Gordon's *T.S. Eliot : An Imperfect Life* of Eliot reading a poem to the assembled women of Shamley Green, where he stayed during World War Two. A maid listens to him attentively, as do Lina Mirrlees and her sister, who sit with their heads high and eyes bright, like two proud old eagles. Hope sits with her head down over her sewing, her hair up in a bun, looking dowdy and ordinary. It is a long fall from being a hummingbird and a cross between a pixie and a genius, to third woman in your mother's house.[140]

Exactly when Mirrlees met T.S. Eliot is not known. They were both among the first to be published by the Woolfs' Hogarth Press, and they traveled in the same literary circles. By 1930, Hope and Tom were established friends, but they may have known each other for far longer. In 1926, Harrison wrote to Prince Mirsky that she'd been reading Eliot "under compulsion of Hope."[141] In 1936, Eliot inscribed a copy of Tennyson "H. Hope Mirrlees from T. Stearns Eliot,"[142] a dry joke suggesting a friendly intimacy. She was certainly more than just an acquaintance. When Eliot decided to separate from his first wife, Vivienne, she was one of the few friends he had who was willing to look in on her from time to time, to keep track of her and make sure she was all right.

For a BBC program on Eliot, first aired in 1971, Hope was to recall how a perfectly ordinary remark could provoke from Vivienne the most extraordinary response : "She gave the impression of absolute terror of a person who's seen a hideous goblin, a goblin ghost. . . . Her face was all drawn and white, with wild, frightened, angry eyes. An overintensity over nothing, you see. Supposing you were to say to her, 'Oh, will you have some more cake ?' she'd say : 'What's that ? What do you mean ? What do you say that for ?' She was terrifying. At the end of an hour I was absolutely exhausted, sucked dry. And I said to myself : Poor Tom, this is enough ! But she was his muse all the same."[143]

In 1941, Woolf wrote a friend that Tom Eliot was "domesticating with Hope Mirrlees : spiritually, of course."[144] In October of the previous year, Eliot had become a paying guest at Mrs. Mirrlees' house in Shamley Green, a village within commuting distance of London. His biographies usually present this stay as being arranged in order to provide him a refuge from the Blitz. Since he spent three days a week in London working as an editor for Faber and Faber and one night a week on the fire watch, however, it's clear that what he was seeking was not so much safety as the tranquility in which to compose his poems.

The house, officially named "Shamley Woods" but unofficially "the Shambles," was situated high above the village at the top of a steep hill, and held not only Hope, her mother, and her aunt, but also evacuees from Wandsworth and Barking, for a total of between eighteen and twenty-two women and children, and only one other adult male, the ancient gardener, Mr. Turner, who was afraid of mice and wrote letters of condolence to the royal family and saved the acknowledgments as testimonials, though the occasional husband popped up on Saturday nights. The Shambles was large and comfortable, with a spectacular view of the surrounding countryside, and had its own cow, so that its inhabitants did not lack for milk and butter.

It was a pleasant situation for Eliot, to be a renowned poet in a household of women who pampered and looked after him. He read *Uncle Remus* aloud to them, and when he finished a new poem ("Dry Salvages" and "East Coker" among them), they were his first audience.[145]

Eliot took long solitary walks, and enjoyed the domestic comedy of Hope's aunt cadging cigarettes from him in private,[146] the local Field Marshall (Margaret Behrens, a now-forgotten writer of E. F. Benson-ish novels set in Scotland) hunting for her Pekinese, which was perpetually out chasing rabbits after dark, and serious conversations about whether one's pets would be waiting in the afterlife.[147] At Hope's insistence, he finally got around to reading *Huckleberry Finn*,[148] and through her sister, Margot Coker, he was introduced to the fox-hunting set who gathered at Bicester House. The entire family — Hope, her brother General W.H.B. Mirrlees, the Cokers, and her mother — all became warm friends of Eliot. Years later, Eliot would write to Hope, "You would be surprised to know how often, and how wistfully, I think of Shamley from time to time. I think of Shamley (though I never want to re-visit it — I mean Shamley then) — and when I say Shamley I mean "Shamley Wood" — and what Mappie made it, as "home" : the nearest I have had since I was a boy. And it may be that I did there what will be regarded as my best work. And I think of Mappie, for a moment every day — as you say, in eternity."[149]

In 1948, Lina Mirrlees died. "Mrs. Mirrlees is a remarkable woman,"[150] T.S. Eliot used to tell his friends with great emphasis, and surely she must have been. Though she did not fare well in her four (mutually contradictory) appearances in her daughter's novels, a woman who would invite Alfred North Whitehead and A. E. Housman to a dinner party in order to entertain a guest, traveled the world, kept households on two continents, earned the admiration of Eliot, and was explicitly among those who inspired Whitehead to write that "uneducated clever women, who have seen much of the world, are in middle life so much the most cultured part of our community,"[151] deserves a better accounting than can be given here.

With her mother gone, Hope had nothing to hold her in England.[152] She went to Paris and then to Egypt, and then moved to the university town of Stellenbosch in the Cape of Good Hope, South Africa. "So Hope returned to her own Cape," she wrote in a poem expressing her heartfelt if rather superficial love of her new home. There she stayed for fifteen years, returning to England for holidays and occasionally traveling to America.[153] The year after Hope's departure, a cookbook which Mrs. Mirrlees had spent much of her life assembling was finished and posthumously published by her daughter Margot. *Wishful Cooking* by Emily Lina Mirrlee[154] and Margaret Rosalys Coker came out from Faber and Faber, perhaps at the doing of Margot's good friend, Tom Eliot.[155] It contained many recipes for dishes requiring ingredients which in the postwar rationing of 1949 were simply unobtainable. Whence the name. Brief biographical notes at the end at the end of the book detailed the authors' relationships with one hundred and ten people (friends, employees, and relations) who contributed recipes. Hope, who was never particularly close to her sister, was not among them.[156]

A lmost nothing is retrievable of Hope's life in South Africa. Apparently, she did not do much. But she loved the Cape in spring : the sight of herds of Jersey cows feeding among lilies, with egrets on their backs, the smell of freesia, the clarity of the stars at night, the changeless ritual of the mountains turning colors, the black nymphs dressed as bright as flowers, carrying sheaves of poinsettia leaves in their arms. She wrote a poem about all this, entitled "Sickness and Recovery at the Cape of Good Hope in Spring." It was occasioned by an illness that brought her to the Volkshospital and almost killed her. But it is hard not to read into it a sickness and renunciation of her former life in Europe.

This poem was included in an uncopyrighted chapbook of eight poems entitled simply *Poems* which Mirrlees self-published in 1963 in Cape Town. The booklet was later expanded as *Moods and Tensions : Seventeen Poems*, also privately printed, undated, and not copyrighted, with inconsistent corrections in Hope Mirrlees' hand. It was re-published in 1976 by Amate Press, Oxford, in a more polished edition with an introduction by Raymond Mortimer, rudimentary illustrations, and (she had learned from having her novel published without her permission in America) a copyright notice. Though a decade had gone by since the previous publication, only four new poems were added.

The poetry itself is very much the work of a dilettante. It is perhaps cruel to say that the poems contain a few good lines. But it is fair as well. "Bertha frightens Miss Bates" is of some interest to the genre reader, in that it recounts the visit of a fairy-in-disguise to a Jane Austen village as neat and tidy as a Delft plate, carrying a basket containing drugged buns and

> . . . eerie things, half-ballad and half-flower,
> Meadowsweet, lords and ladies, passion fruit,
> The deadly nightshade and the insane root,
> Such things as grow and twine in Proserpina's bower . . .

This irruption of Faerie into the mundane comes calling on Miss Bates, terrifying the poor woman and turning her house Gothic : old Mrs. Bates, sitting in the chimney nook, grins like a witch, the grey polly becomes a bright macaw . . .

> And cosy pussy on the worsted mat
> Turned to 'a silken-haired Angora cat'

Then the crayon sketch of Jane, in omen of a coming death, falls from the wall. But who is Jane ? Jane Fairfax, from *Emma* ? Jane Austen herself ? The poem provides no answers, though "our poor friend, still sobbing, 'My *dear* Jane !' " hints that it may be Jane Harrison. Bertha — the name is that of the Norse goddess of spinning — leaves, and the drugged buns are eaten.

> And with the first taste, prophecies of woe
> Melted as magically as April snow.

The discarded flowers blow through the village visiting terror and ecstasy and beauty, disturbing dreams, the Comus-rout, and Apocalyptic frenzy upon the characters from Austen's *Emma*. All these, and the fair that the children find in Donwell Wood with "real winged horses for the roundabout," could have been lifted directly from *Lud-in-the-Mist*. There ensues an "Envoy." Emma herself, present in but untouched by the first part of the poem, is judged stronger than the forces of Faerie because she possesses "A conscience exquisitely poised." Because of this, she is made

> . . . not merely sane and sound
> But pure enough to wear, one day, the Morning Star.[157]

Faerie and Heaven have been weighed in the balance, and Mirrlees has come down firmly on the side of Christianity. It is purely speculation on my part that this slight work might be all that remains of Hope Mirrlees' fourth novel.

Two of the three chapbooks end with her weakest work, "A Doggerel Epitaph for my Little Dog, Sally."[158] The third ends with eight sentimental lines about her mother's dead maid, titled "Jesus Wept." Mirrlees' retreat from modernism and the avant-garde was complete.

Meanwhile, she had two biographies to work on.

Biography is the White Man's Graveyard for a working writer. The work expands to fill as much time and energy as one will give it. So it did with Hope. What time she did not spend on the vaporware Harrison book, she sank into her second project : a biography of Sir Robert Bruce Cotton, the Elizabethan antiquarian whose collection of manuscripts included the Lindisfarne Gospels, two of the contemporary exemplifications of the Magna Carta and the only surviving manuscript of *Beowulf*.

In this project Mirrlees was encouraged by T.S. Eliot who, in a series of letters extending over decades, revealed himself as the kindest, gentlest, and assuredly most patient of editors.

A Fly in Amber : Being an Extravagant Biography of the Romantic Antiquary Sir Robert Bruce Cotton (the title is the best thing about it) was first presented to Faber and Faber as being all-but-complete and needing only minor changes in 1946, but somehow it always and forever seemed to need just a few more months' work. It was finally published in 1962, with a foreword thanking Eliot "who has read three redactions of the book (he calls it 'Penelope's web' !) And without whose encouragement I might have lacked the heart to finish it." Learned, dry, difficult, and exhibiting not one drop of pity toward the reader, it is in fact only the first half of the intended biography.[159]

Here (brace yourself) is a perfectly typical paragraph :
So Cotton was the one-eyed man who rules in the kingdom of the blind. Genealogy, to be sure, is one of the less important branches of history, and Elizabethan heralds were both ignorant and credulous. Nevertheless it is startling to discover that Cotton knew less about his wife's family, the Brocases, than we do. Presumably he shared their own belief that they were of Norman descent, a belief confirmed in the eighteenth century by Nichols who informs us in his Leicestershire that 'Sir Bernard Brocas, Knight, came into England with William the Conqueror 1066, under whom he was a great commander'. But we now know that they were a Gascon family who did not settle in England till the reign of Edward III. And greatly though Cotton valued his descent from the Bruces, for at least half his life he was mistaken as to the maiden name of the ancestress to whom he owed it, and also as to the way in which Conington had come to him. His friend Nicholas Charles, the Lancaster Herald who, as Camden's deputy, made the 1613 Visitation of Huntingdon, describes the royal blood-donor as the daughter and heir (filia et haeres) of Robert de Wesenham, whereas we know that she was really the latter's grand-daughter and by birth a Folville of Reresby. And it was not to her but to her son that, in a will made in 1460, Robert de Wesenham bequeathed Conington. We presume that Charles's

findings had been submitted to Cotton and approved by him, as the manuscript in which they are recorded is preserved in his library. And yet he owned Folville Charters, and perhaps it was thanks to them that the Lancaster Herald, shortly after his visitation, seems to have been assailed by doubts on the matter. He says in a letter to Cotton, 'as for the Cottons of the chevron between the eagles, I think it was no match with Wesenham but rather with the Folvilles.'[160]

What Mirrlees intended is best explained in an essay she wrote for *The Nation & Athenaeum* titled "Listening in to the Past." After a digressive opening in which she comments that "a kaleidoscope is the prettiest toy ever invented, and the most entertaining of all the thieves of time," she comes to her subject :

> If the time ever comes when we can listen in to the past, I shall immediately order a wireless, though this will be due more to my love of a kaleidoscope than to my love of the past. My knowledge of the relation between sound-waves and ether-waves is of the vaguest, nor do I know anything about electricity, magnetism, or the Quantum Theory, nevertheless I am sure it will be very difficult to control the old fragments of human speech blown in from the waste lands of the universe to be lost again for another thousand years. No, it will be an aural kaleidoscope, rather than a lesson in history : disparate fragments of Cockney, Egyptian, Babylonian, Provençal, ever forming into new patterns for the ear, but not the mind.

Following which, she provides a kaleidoscopic series of images — the elf-bound ghost of a soldier, the passion of Queen Mary, a little boy carrying the head and one leg of a conspirator to St. Andrews — taken from Elizabethan history, and continues :

> There is a particularly glorious kind of kaleidoscope for which you yourself provide the materials for the patterns. Under the lens there is a little tray, and on this you place any thin brightly colored scraps you can lay hands on . . . the silver paper off chocolates, for instance, the petals of flowers, and so on.

And, as you gradually add to this collection of scraps, you sometimes find — from the addition, say, of a purplish-brown element given by a wallflower's petal or from the brilliant blue of a butterfly's wing, rifled from your childhood's collection — that both the colours and design of the patterns suddenly become much more beautiful.[161]

By example and implication, her aesthetic strategy for *A Fly in Amber* — the kaleidoscopic juxtaposition of beautiful fragments and disparate voices — is spelled out here as clearly as it ever can be. It was not, however, a strategy with much hope for popular acclaim. The book was unfavorably reviewed and the second volume — of which, Margaret Ellis wrote, "It is a very 'extravagant' biography, being possibly even more diffuse than the first volume"[162] — though completed, has never been published.

Mirrlees returned to England in 1963 — primarily, according to family, because she couldn't stand the apartheid system — and bought a house in Headington, Oxford,[163] thus putting an end to her peripatetic lifestyle, if not her essential eccentricity. Catriona Kelly wrote that "My mother gave a vivid description of her as rather square, chain-smoking, with a very deep voice in which she used to cajole her dogs (mostly pugs, I think) : she would stand at the bottom of the stairs and call out : 'Tuwit tuwoo Mary dog, tuwit tuwoo Ma-ry !' "[164]

In 1969 or '70, through the intercession of Mary Lascelles, she acquired an amanuensis to help her research the second Cotton book in the person of Margaret Ellis, who described her work routine as follows :

I did research for her partly here in Oxford in the Bodleian and partly in the British Museum. I was also — fairly frequently — called in by her housekeeper, Dorothy Edmonds, to help with what was known as 'paper chases' when manuscript material was lost or papers became muddled. Work always took place in the afternoon, punctuated by tea, served promptly at four, and later by the arrival of the drinks trolley ; brandy for Miss Mirrlees and dry martini for me. I fed bread and butter at tea time and ice cubes at six to the pug, Fred, who always joined us in 'the book room' ! We became over the years very close.[165]

John Saunders, Mirrlees' first cousin once removed, met her at Bicester House. His mother had spoken warmly of Margot, Reay, and most particularly Lina, but described Hope, who had apparently been cruelly contemptuous of her shy and impoverished younger cousin, as "beautiful but mad." He himself wrote, "My first impression was of a semi-invalid — a cross between Miss Havisham and Harpo Marx. It was soon clear that she moved between lethargy and an extraordinary anarchic energy — which came over at times like a sophisticated form of Tourette's syndrome."

Saunders recorded three incidents from their first Christmas at Bicester House that capture something of her style and unpredictability. As they drove up the drive :

Hope ordered the driver to stop. 'Look', she said, 'isn't that a beautiful sight'. Two men, apparently 'servants' in the Bicester's employ, were clearing away mounds of snow. The loveliness, I was to learn, had nothing to do with the freshness of the snow but with the glimpsing of the last vestiges of servitude.

After lunch they underwent the "ceremony of the Christmas Cards" which was an annual tradition :

Hope made Margot accompany her along the lines of rows of cards on display. One by one they categorised them. Most (including mine) were dismissed a 'HIDGEOUS'. A few were deemed 'nicely, nicely'. The gems of the collection, generally featuring Rob Red Breasts, were given the highest accolade, 'FRABJOUS'. Margot acted as a moderate moderator, apparently knowing 'the rules' but generally trying to raise rather than lower Hope's classifications.

And, least attractively :

> Margot had a small retinue of her own 'servants', including a cook, several gardeners and an elderly maid. The maid who had worked for the Coker family all her life, was named Lily Hole. That evening, when Lily waited on us at table, Hope suddenly accosted her, 'Well, if it isn't Hole, Lily, Lily Hole. How are you Lilious Bilious, Bilious Hole ?' — she asked, chuckling at her 'joke'.

She was not invariably glum and rude. When the mood took her, she could be charming, gracious, and a witty conversationalist. "From time to time Hope hosted small parties of my graduate acquaintances," Saunders wrote. "It soon became clear that she was very fond of most of the men but had little time for my women friends, particularly those who might have been classified as 'blue stockings'." He tried to introduce her to work of contemporary poets like Hughes, Plath and Larkin, but she would have none of it. And yet he learned to his amazement that "on one occasion she had visited London (staying at the Basil Street Hotel) and had attended and much enjoyed the controversial musical 'Hair' — featuring full frontal male nudity."[166]

By this time Hope was very much dependent upon her sister Margot. Somewhere along the line her money had dwindled away. "Miss Mirrlees felt, towards the end of her life, that her circumstances — although she pretended not to be sure what was meant by a 'fixed income' — were uncomfortably straitened," Margaret Ellis wrote. With the help of Valerie Eliot, she sold most of her letters to American libraries.

Late in her life, there was a resurgence of interest in Hope Mirrlees, due entirely to the 1970 reprint by Ballantine Books of *Lud-in-the-Mist*. In his introduction, Lin Carter spoke for many when he said that though he was a lifelong fantasy reader, he'd been astonished to learn of the book's existence. He also noted he'd been unable to locate Mirrlees. But he published her book anyway, since it was by the American copyright laws of the time in the public domain.

Carter can't have tried very hard to find Mirrlees, for she was then living in "The Firs," a book-filled house in Oxford on a hill above the Isis. Certainly she noticed him, or rather his activities, for that same year, after four and a half decades of silence, there was a flurry of correspondence between her agent and Collins, reverting rights to *Lud-in-the-Mist*. She had the satisfaction of arranging for an authorized British reprint of her novel in 1972, and of having at least one overawed young scholar seek her out and ask naïve questions. Suzanne Henig's article on Mirrlees in the *Virginia Woolf Quarterly* is a rare source of biographical material, but one can't help feeling here and there that Hope has succumbed to temptation and is having her on shamelessly.

Far better to recall her as her nephew does : "I remember her as an old lady living in a nice house in Oxford surrounded with books from floor to ceiling and laughing at her age," he wrote. "Hopie did put on weight as she got older, it's true, and lost her looks, except for her beautiful eyes." But she had a wicked sense of humor, and a wonderful ability to make the moment special. Once, when he was driving her somewhere in France, she glanced in the rear-view mirror and remarked, "It's all fading behind me, like my checquered past."[167]

On August 1, 1978, Hope Mirrlees died. "I don't think she was ever ill during her whole life, not even a cold, and when she was 98, she simply went to sleep in the arms of the Lord. I had promised her housekeeper and doctor large sums if they could keep her going just two more years until the full 100, but to no avail,"[168] her nephew wrote, and though his math was a bit off (she died at age 91), the love she inspired in him shines from his words. She was cremated and her name added to the family memorial in the churchyard by Glasgow Cathedral. Her will stated, "I desire and direct my trustees to see that my body shall be cremated and that my ashes are scattered on the grave of my dog 'Fred' in the grounds of my home 'the Firs' aforesaid," and presumably this was done.[169]

There were no obituaries.

In the aftermath of her death, her young cousin John Graham Saunders set to work with Margaret Ellis, to sort through her papers and books. They had barely begun when there was a surprise visit by Mirrlees' third literary executor. As Saunders recounts it, "One enigmatic event has stayed with me. Before we had a chance to decide on our procedures, Valerie Eliot raided Hope's desk and found a batch of letters from Mary Lascelles, a close friend, a spinsterly Oxford Don, reputed to be of highly aristocratic breeding. 'Hope told me to take these,' Valerie said, thrusting the letters into a bag and ensuring that we didn't have a chance to read them. Margaret and I learned that Hope had, with Valerie's assistance, sold most of her most interesting letters to American universities — which reminds me that any wealth she had inherited had been mismanaged, leaving her relatively hard-up in her last years."[170]

The bulk of Hope Mirrlees' estate was left to her housekeeper as compensation for caring for her during her declining years. Several small individual items, including a "fly in amber" (which her nephew insists was actually an ant) were left to various friends and family members. A pencil sketch of Jane Ellen Harrison by Theo van Rysselberghe was bequeathed to the National Portrait Gallery.

As of the time of this book, *Lud-in-the-Mist* is undergoing a second rediscovery. In London, Millennium has recently republished it in a handsome trade paperback (with an evocative cover by David Wyatt that was originally a painting of Tolkien's Rivendell) as part of its Fantasy Masterworks line, and there are several small press publications as well — for it does remain in the public domain in the United States if not in Britain. It has also has been translated as *Flucht ins Feenland*, "Flight into Fairyland," in Germany, and *Entrebrumas*, "Inside Mist," in Spain. The critical reception for all of these has been warmly positive. Most recently, *Paris* has been reprinted with an introduction and exposition by Julia Briggs in *Gender in Modernism*, edited by Bonnie Kime Scott and published by the University of Illinois. Though Leonard Woolf wanted to reprint it in 1946, Mirrlees regretted some of its content and refused him permission ; thus, this is the first time this poem has appeared in print intact since its initial publication in an edition of 175 copies.

The number of fantasists who consider Hope Mirrlees an important influence is surprisingly large. Elizabeth Hand has compared Mirrlees to the Velvet Underground, of whose first album it has often been said that it sold only a hundred copies but everyone who bought one went on to start a band. That influence, covert though it is, continues to grow.

The implicit story that Virginia Woolf related in her diary and letters was one of failure, of brilliant promise come to naught in a flutter of unwritten letters, poems never begun, literary boats and buses missed, friendships declined, and diaries not kept. Still, there is *Paris.* There is *Lud-in-the-Mist.* Each work has its passionate advocates, and if those two groups of partisans neither overlap nor fully understand each other, nevertheless they exist. It is entirely possible that Hope Mirrlees' literary reputation, at one point virtually nonexistent, may yet rise like the phoenix from the ashes.

NOTES :

1 The Mirrlees clan (variant spellings include Mirrilees, Merrylee, Mirrielees, etc.) were originally "tacksmen" or farmers living near Glasgow. The name, which probably means "a happy meadow near a pond," is derived from an ancestral dwelling-place not far from the Antonine Wall.

2 Catriona Kelly, private correspondence. I suppose I really ought to put "[sic]" after one of the diminutives of Hope's name. However, I can't decide which is correct and which not.

3 In the eighteenth century, Charles Mirrlees was a weaver and a merchant. His eldest son, William, entered into the Incorporation of Hammermen — metal-workers — first as a saddler and then a manufacturer of the frames on which saddles were made, and later as a cutler and surgical instrument maker. He earned enough to invest in a steamship line, and become a member of the Board of the Clydesdale Bank. William's son, also named William, inherited the family business, engaged in numerous property transactions, and expanded the leather working operations. William junior's third son, James Buchanan Mirrlees, was the great success of the family. His estate house, "Redlands," near Glasgow later became first a women's hospital, and then the National Training Centre for the Scottish Ambulance Service. For more detailed information, see Derek A. Dow, *Redlands House : Hospital, Hostel and Home*, (Paisley : Scottish Ambulance Service, 1985).

4 Mr. Mirrlees was trained as an engineer in Glasgow. He also served a lieutenant in the Natal Mounted Rifles during the Zulu War, and had to spend several years in the hospital after being wounded by an exploding ammunition wagon. He was the editor and owner of a weekly newssheet in South Africa called "the Mosquito" and kept a large house full of servants at "Amanzimayama" near the sugar estate, a few miles north of Durban.

5 Or so Virginia Woolf testified. (Virginia Woolf, *The Letters of Virginia Woolf* : Volume Three : 1925-1930, 1980, Nigel Nicolson & Joanne Trautmann, eds., NY : Harcourt Brace Jovanovich, pp. 200-201) Mirrlees' nephew Robin, however, wrote me that "Even if Hopie owned various cars I never saw her driving one, and I think she generally got other people to drive for her."

6 Julia Briggs' entry in the *Dictionary of National Biography* characterizes the Moncrieffs at this time as "cultivated Edinburgh lawyers."

7 "She used to go around Africa on a bicycle, back when that sort of thing simply wasn't done. This was a hundred years ago, when the continent was half-wild. She was quite a character," said Robin Mirrlees of his great-aunt. She was also, he testified, an early suffragist. Much of her life was spent in the Pyrenees; she was among the last Britons to be evacuated from Bordeaux in June 1940.

8 Virginia Woolf, *The Diary of Virginia Woolf*, Volume Two : 1920-1924, Anne Oliver Bell, ed., NY : Harcourt Brace Jovanovich, 197, p. 48. "Sneezer" would be William Henry Buchanan Mirrlees, Hope's brother. In later life, he was usually referred to as Reay, or simply as "the General." His sisters, however, called him "The Sneezer."

9 Robin Mirrlees, private correspondence. Quoted with permission. Count Robin's (at that time, he had not yet asserted his title as Prince of Coronata) first, long letter of reminiscences about his aunt was published, with his permission, as "My Aunt, Hope Mirrlees," in the January 2002 issue of *The New York Review of Science Fiction*.

10 There is a family tradition that she taught herself Greek. I have found no independent confirmation of this. Whatever the truth, it is a good indication of how highly those who knew her esteemed Mirrlees' intellectual prowess.

11 Newnham College : affiliated with Cambridge University; for women. Organized in 1873, it has been a college since 1875. In 1881 some privileges of the university were open to women; degrees have been given only since 1921. Stewart and Peacock stated that Mirrlees began Newnham in 1909. However, I am assured by the college that the correct dates are 1910-1913.

12 E.M. Butler, quoted in Jesse G. Stewart, *Jane Ellen Harrison : a portrait from letters*, (London : The Merlin Press), 1959, p. 174.

13 Raymond Mortimer, introduction, *Moods and Tensions : Seventeen Poems*, (Oxford & Tehran : Amate Press, 1976). Over a quarter century later, Margaret Ellis wrote that she possessed, "a pastel of [Mirrlees] by Simon Busey which shows something of her sense of fun as she is wearing, very prominently, blue stockings!"

14 Woolf, *Letters*, Vol. III, September 1, 1925, p. 200.

15 Woolf, *Diary*, Vol. 4, November 12, 1934, p. 261.

16 Woolf, *Diary*, Vol. I, March 22, 1919, p. 258.

17 Woolf, *Letters*, Vol. II, May 1, 1920, p. 432.

18 However, "Others were not short of criticisms and described her as silly, affected, pretentious, ostentatious, spoiled, mannered, over-refined." (Annabel Robinson, *The Life and Work of Jane Ellen Harrison*, Oxford : Oxford University Press, 2002, p. 236.)

19 Suzanne Henig, "Queen of Lud : Hope Mirrlees," *Virginia Woolf Quarterly* I (1972), p. 10. By the time of the interview, her languages included French, Russian, Greek, Latin, Zulu, Spanish, Arabic, Persian, Italian, and Old Norse. And, of course, English. It is possible her Zulu was not comprehensive, given Henig's remark that "She can still speak the native African clicking language, though is reluctant to do so."

20 In fact, her father bought the lease of a house at 11 Cranmer Road, Cambridge, from Alfred North Whitehead, in order to be near her, while simultaneously commissioning the building of a permanent house, "Mount Blow," designed by Sir Edwin Lutyens, nearby at Great Shelford. A family dog named Cranmer (Peacock, p. 109) memorialized the first house. How much time Mirrlees spent at either is uncertain. But in any event, it does not appear that she ever shared lodgings with Harrison in Cambridge.

21 Mary Beard, *The Invention of Jane Harrison*, (Boston : Harvard University Press, 2000), p. 162.

22 Jessie G. Stewart, *Jane Ellen Harrison: a portrait from letters*, (London : The Merlin Press, 1959), p. 147.

23 Equally possible is that they met through Mrs. Patrick Campbell, who was friends with Jane's fellow Cambridge Ritualist, professor Gilbert Murray, in whose plays she sometimes appeared.

24 Robin Mirrlees, telephone conversation. The young man was apparently a sea-captain, rather than an army officer.

25 Robin Mirrlees, *NYRSF*.

26 The two, along with Karin's mother Mary Costelloe, also visited Italy for the usual artistic round of galleries and museums, styling themselves "the aesthetic trio." (Beard, pp. 135-136.)

27 Stewart, p. 156. Whether they succeeded is not known. Robinson records an odd incident in 1914 when Jane "went with Hope Mirrlees's mother Lena [sic] to pour out coffee in a camp at dawn : 'the beauty of the tents in the mist almost undid me — it was so Old Testament — like the hosts of Midian or the children of Israel or something. Why is a host of tents so horribly moving? Is it "tout passe", etc.?'" (Robinson, p. 261)

28 "Their friends nicknamed the Hotel d'Elysée the 'Hotel du Lapin' after a rabbit which lived in a hutch at the bottom of the stairs. The rabbit would have appealed to Harrison's love of animals, but others of her friends found it insupportable and unhygienic, and when Jessie Crum (Stewart) visited them there her father, to Harrison's regret, insisted it be removed." (Robinson, p. 265)

29 Woolf, *Diary*, Vol. I, September 8, 1918, p. 191.

30 Anthony Powell, *Faces in My Time*, (NY : Holt, Rinehart and Winston, 1981), pp. 181-2.

31 Woolf, *Letters*, Vol. III, February 5, 1925, p. 164.

32 Sandra J. Peacock, *Jane Ellen Harrison : the mask and the self*, (New Haven : Yale University Press, 1988), p. 111.

33 Beard, p. 134. The dissection of Peacock's misreading is to be found on pp. 208-209, note 10.

34 Woolf, *Letters*, Vol. II, September 24, 1919, p. 391.

35 Jane Ellen Harrison, *Reminiscences of a Student's Life*, (London : Hogarth Press, 1925), p.21.

36 Julia Briggs, "The Wives of Herr Bear," *London Review of Books*, September 21, 2000, pp. 24-25.

37 Mirrlees, *Madeleine, One of Love's Jansenists*, (London : W. Collins Sons & Co., 1919), p. 157. For providing me with a photocopy of this all-but-unobtainable book, and other materials as well, I am particularly grateful to Juliet O'Keefe.

38 Robin Mirrlees, *NYRSF*. It is also worth noting that Mirrlees was part of a remarkable generation of British women who had to come to grips with the fact that something like one third of all the marriageable men had just died in World War One. There was at that time nothing extraordinary about a young woman simply being unmarried.

39 Martha Vicinus, private correspondence. Similarly, in her biography of Jane Harrison, Robinson writes of Mirrlees, "The record has not been kind to her. 'Not my favourite lady' was the instant verdict of one woman who had known Mirrlees," (p. 235). A footnote identifies the woman as Jean Pace, the daughter of her old schoolmate, Jessie Crum.

40 "She often called her stuffed bear 'the Old One', or 'O. O.' as he appears on many postcards, and never allowed anyone to call him a teddy-bear : he was her 'authentic plaything'. At other times he was 'Herr Professor', perhaps with echoes of Brunn. He had spectacles and an umbrella but no other clothing. Apparently he had only one good eye." (Robinson, pp. 238-9)

41 Beard, p. 135; Peacock reports the same letter as saying that the Bear's younger wife is not a "comic cub." Hope's handwriting was not the clearest in the world. Possibly, her mentor's was not much better.

42 Peacock, p. 112. Beard also records a version of this same note, with minor variants.

43 Harrison, p. 41.

44 Stewart, p. 178.

45 Harrison, p. 90.

46 Stewart, p. 174.

47 Alice B. Toklas, *What is Remembered*, (NY : Holt, Rinehart and Winston, 1963), p. 83.

48 Seventy items of correspondence from Mirrlees to Morrell are archived in the Ottoline Morrell Collection in the Harry Ransom Research Center at the University of Texas in Austin. However, like the letters from T.S. Eliot to Hope Mirrlees preserved at the University of Maryland at College Park they are mostly "bread and butter" notes, though they contain several interesting snippets of information.

49 Woolf, *Diary*, Vol. I, August 24, 1918, pp. 185-186.

50 Woolf, *Letters*, Vol. II, February 16, 1919, p. 331.

51 Woolf, *Diary*, Vol. I, February 25, 1919, p. 244.

52 Woolf, *Diary*, Vol. I, March 22, 1919, p. 244.

53 Woolf, *Letters*, Vol. II, August 12, 1919, p. 383.

54 Woolf, *Letters*, Vol. II, August 17, 1919, pp. 384-385.

55 "Hail Paris, full of grace," a graceful pun on the beginning of a quintessentially Catholic prayer.

56 Julia Briggs, private correspondence.

57 For a more detailed and insightful analysis of the poem, I highly recommend " 'Printing Hope' : Virginia Woolf, Hope Mirrlees, and the Iconic Imagery of Paris" by Julia Briggs, in *Woolf in the Real World : Selected Papers from the Thirteenth International Conference on Virginia Woolf*, Karen V. Kukil, ed., Clemson, SC : Clemson University Digital Press, 2005, and "Modernism's Lost Hope," chapter 8 of *Reading Virginia Woolf* (Edinburgh University Press, Edinburgh : 2006), also by Julia Briggs.

58 The poem was written mostly when Eliot was at Lausanne in the winter of 1921. It has been suggested that Ezra Pound, who worked with Eliot to edit and revise *The Waste Land*, may have read *Paris* and so passed its influence indirectly to Eliot. Both lines of influence, it should be emphasized, are at this time purely speculative.

59 Suzanne Henig, "Queen of Lud : Hope Mirrlees," *Virginia Woolf Quarterly* I (1972), p. 13. There are many typos in Henig's article ; the correct title of this poem is *Le Cap de Bonne-Espérance*.

60 Charles Du Bos, *Approximations* (4me serie), (Paris : R.A. Correa, 1930), p. 922. Jean Paul Sartre characterized this essay as "a bad introduction to a bad book." (*The War Diaries of Jean-Paul Sartre*, NY : Pantheon Books, 1984, p. 276.)

61 Bruce Bailey, "A Note on *The Waste Land* and Hope Mirrlees' *Paris*," *T S. Eliot Newsletter*, Department of English, York University, Fall 1974. Like almost everyone else who has considered the possibility, Bailey was intuitively certain that an influence was inescapable.

62 According to Briggs : "The marked-up sheet of page proofs of Paris (pp. 13, 14, 15) are in the E. J. Pratt Library of Victoria University, Toronto ... Woolf's letter to Mirrlees in *A Change of Perspective : Letters, vol. III, 1923-28* (1977), p. 3, [6 January 1923]." The quote is taken from "Writing by Numbers : An Aspect of Woolf's Revisionary Practice", *Variants* 4, 2005, pp. 169-170.

63 When, more than half a century later, Mirrlees revised *Paris* for its first reprint in the *Virginia Woolf Quarterly*, in addition to removing lines she then considered blasphemous, she took the opportunity to change these problematic words to "Japanese" and "Negro." While the wisdom of revising published work can be debated (one short section rewritten to bring the poem into line with her conversion to Catholicism is in glaring violation of the format of the rest), it is pleasing to learn that the originals were sins of ignorance, rather than of malice.

64 Henig, pp. 11-12. The date mentioned, 1554, should be 1654.

65 In her madness, Madeleine becomes the god of her own pocket universe, which (since earlier in times of distress she gave in to a self-invented frenzied form of dance) neatly recapitulated Jane Harrison's theories about religion being born out of ecstatic ritual.

66 Julia Briggs, "Hope Mirrlees and Continental Modernism", Bonnie Kime Scott, ed., *Gender in Modernism : New Geographies, Complex Intersections*, (University of Illinois Press: 2007), p. 266.

67 Julia Briggs, *Reading Virginia Woolf*, p. 83.

68 Mirrlees, *Madeleine*, pp. vii-viii.

69 *TLS*, October 9, 1919, 547. Other reviews were more positive. R. Brimley

Johnson dedicated a chapter of *Some Contemporary Authors (Women)* to it the next year. The quality of his analysis, however, can be judged by the fact that I was unable to find anything in it worth quoting. Mirrlees herself, in later years, quietly dropped the book from her bibliography and identified herself as being the author of two novels.

70 Katherine Mansfield, letter, recipient unrecorded, October 21, 1919 (*The Letters of Katherine Mansfield,* Vol. I, ed. John Middleton Murray, Constable and Company Limited, 1930, p. 261).

71 Beard, p. 214. This is Mirrlees' characterization, taken from her unpublished biographical notes in the Harrison Archive at Newnham. The man was the scholar and poet Francis Cornford, who broke Harrison's heart by marrying another and younger woman.

72 Robinson, p. 291.

73 "Jane Harrison died at 11 Mecklenburgh Street on 15 April 1928. Her will, a final clue to her relationship with Mirrlees, left everything to her niece, Marion Harrison," Robinson wrote on page 304, deftly implying something for which there is no other evidence.

74 Virginia Woolf, *Letters,* Vol. III, July 30, 1923, pp. 58-59.

75 In fact, Harrison felt that the Roman Mass was not ritualistic enough. In *Reminiscences of a Student's Life,* she (apparently in the belief that the Orthodox Mass was the more primitive and thus authentic form) stated that it should be performed behind a curtain, at the end of which a priest would come out and inform the congregation that the ritual had been enacted.

76 Woolf, *Letters,* Vol. III, January 6, 1923, pp. 3-4.

77 Robinson, p. 294. Practically anything is conceivable, of course. However, this public denial of an interior life seems to be of a piece with Mirrlees' extremely developed sense of privacy. The lady liked to play her cards close to the chest.

78 Gerald Stanton Smith, *D. S. Mirsky : A Russian-English Life 1890-1939,* New York : Oxford University Press, 2000, p. 98.

79 Catriona Kelly, private correspondence.

80 Smith, *D. S. Mirsky*, p. 149.

81 Marilyn Schwinn-Smith, "Bears in Bloomsbury," in *Virginia Woolf : Three Centenary Celebrations*, Maria Cândida Zamith and Luísa Flora, eds., Porto : Universidade do Porto, Faculdade de Letras, 2007. It's entirely possible the money came from Hope.

82 Catriona Kelly, private correspondence.

83 Woolf, *Letters*, Vol. III, January 6, 1923, p. 4.

84 Harrison, p. 11.

85 Christopher Isherwood, *Diaries* : Volume I : 1939-1960 (NY : HarperCollins, 1996), p. 483.

86 Mirrlees, *Counterplot*, pp. 101-102.

87 The ancestral home of Mirrlees' brother-in-law, Major Aubrey Coker. It will reappear in this narrative. Catriona Kelly describes it as "a spectacularly beautiful Georgian house, not that big (maybe four or five large rooms on each floor, plus attics and outbuildings?), with beautiful long windows on to the walled garden," and an orangery. However, she adds, "It wasn't, by the way, at all like a fairy-tale cottage in the woods - it was pure Jane Austen." Located on the site of the manor-house of the nuns of Markyate, the house was enlarged in the eighteenth and nineteenth centuries. It has been in the Coker family since 1584.

88 Mirrlees, *Counterplot*, p. 146.

89 Mirrlees, *Counterplot*, p. 102. The reference to Dionysus and Apollo is almost certainly a nod to Friedrich Nietzsche, whose work had a strong influence on Jane Ellen Harrison.

90 Mirrlees, *Counterplot*, p. 334.

91 Robin Mirrlees, *NYRSF*.

92 For this sampling of writers who may well have influenced Mirrlees' writing,

either in a positive or a negative sense, I am indebted to John Clute, who provided me with both suggestions and annotations. Whatever Mirrlees may or may not have read, there was definitely something in the air. Sylvia Townsend Warner's first novel, *Lolly Willowes* (1927), has the spooky jangle of an untuned harp at one end and a carousel at the other. Had it been published a year later, the nod to *Lud* would be irrefutable; as it is, there was not the time for the one book to influence the other. Nor is there evidence that STW ever met or even heard of HM. She was, however, like Mirrlees, a great admirer of Alexei Remizov.

93 "Had Mirrlees read Dunsany?" Darrell Schweitzer wrote recently. "Yes, certainly. A phrase like 'the Debatable Hills' could have come right out of *The Book of Wonder*." ("Tapdancing on the Shoulders of Giants : Gaiman's Stardust and its Antecedents", *The New York Review of Science Fiction*, May 2006 : Number 123, Vol. 18, no. 9, p. 19.) It's a plausible conclusion. Dunsany was a popular writer, and it feels intuitively sound. The scholar in me, however, devoutly wishes there were documentation.

94 I owe profound thanks to Greer Gilman for locating a copy of this long-forgotten essay in the Harvard Library. It is quite possible there are more of Mirrlees' writings available only in French.

95 Jane Austen, Madame Blavatsky, Robert Browning, Defoe, Dostoevski, Dumas pere, George Eliot, Flaubert, Gogol, Herrick, Horace, Joubert, Lamb, Walter Savage Landor, William Morris, Saint Paul, Plato, Pope, Proust, Pushkin, Rabelais, Sir Walter Scott, Shakespeare, Swift, Tennyson, Tolstoy, Virgil, Oscar Wilde, and P.G. Wodehouse. Wodehouse, who died in 1975, only three years short of Mirrlees herself and was, coincidentally, a neighbor of her sister-in-law in France during the Blitzkrieg, was mentioned in a list of things and people that she had heard described as "Shakespearian."

96 Jane Harrison and Hope Mirrlees, trans., *The Book of the Bear* (London: Nonesuch, 1926), x-xi. The book is dedicated "to the GREAT bear."

97 Woolf, *Letters*, Vol. III, April 8, 1925, p. 177.

98 Stewart, p. 195.

99 Beard states that Mirrlees and Harrison returned to London in 1925. Peacock claims they returned in March of 1926, and found the flat in April. Stewart says

only that Jane's two-year term of residency at the American Club ended in the spring of 1925, and that the two women then took an extended vacation. Since all of Harrison's biographers have a demonstrated carelessness in matters of minor fact, the reader is urged to consider all such dates as being provisional, rather than exact. The "mousetrap" comment is taken from Robinson, p. 302.

100 Woolf, *Letters*, Vol. III, February 5, 1925, p. 164.

101 Family lore has it that there was for a time something seriously wrong with Julius and/or his marriage. At this late date, however, nothing remains but speculation.

102 Margot doubtless deserved better. A more nuanced sketch of her personality is given by Catriona Kelly, her cousin twice removed: "I remember Margot very well myself. I don't think I met her more than at most four of five times, but I remember that she surfaced when my parents did a concert at the Maison Francaise in Oxford and we went out to Bicester House. [. . .] Margot had an old retainer called Lily who had been with her for decades, and also a Spanish couple. There was an extraordinary tea and Margot conversed happily with no concessions to the presence of two children. I was then 15 or 16 I suppose and my sister 13 or 14. I remember that among the things she said was that she needed a 'tame cat' for her dinner parties, 'only it's no use in Oxford! They're all queer in Oxford!' I laughed at this, which she liked. She smoked those Cyprus cigarettes that are almond-shaped cylinders, as though someone had sat on them, which were sent to her by the box as a special order, kept a diary into which she pasted concert programmes etc., and bred geraniums — and when I displayed interest in this she gave me one, called 'Patchwork Quilt', a very elegant variegated one that she'd taken to a show, with pale green leaves and mauve-pink rather reticent flowers, just a few to a stem rather than the florid 'frilly knicker' look you get with the usual pelargonium. She also kept dogs — a rather hysterical Cavalier King Charles that she called Boydikins Boyd and called for in the Hope manner (Boydikins Boydikins Boydikins Bo-OYD!) right up the stairs. I also remember her saying that a friend had visited and brought her husband who had gone mad, and Margot had said, when the husband looked out at the lawn and called out anxiously: 'What's that yacht out there?' 'Oh, people will leave these things lying around, you know!' She drove fast and determinedly from Oxford but used the train to go to London, though she complained that the staff at Marylebone were black, which she didn't mind, 'but they're black and cross!' — which she did." (Private correspondence.) She was also an elegant woman. I have seen a photograph of her standing in the

stable yard with her nephew, Robin Mirrlees, in riding regalia upon his horse. She was wearing a Chanel suit.

103 *Nigella damascena*. Love-in-the-mist has blue or white petals surrounded by lacy bracts (hence the name), and a distinctly gothic pod. It is also sometimes called devil-in-the-bush or devil-in-a-cage. According to the *OED*, "lud" is a variant of "lede," meaning a people or folk, and also of "lide," meaning noise. So the name may be meant to suggest that the city's populace is benighted, clamoring in the fog. Then again, it may not.

104 The minor fall at the end of this paragraph is typical of Mirrlees. In *Rhetorics of Fantasy* (Middleton, CT : Wesleyan University Press, 2008), p. 185, Farah Mendlesohn establishes her technique of building to a climax and then immediately undercutting it with a observation "almost always utterly irrelevant" as a key technique for creating ironic distance.

105 Her mother's maternal great-uncle, Dr. Granville Sharp Pattison, was involved in an infamous body-snatching case while practicing as a surgeon in Edinburgh. (Dow, p. 29.)

106 Neil Gaiman, introduction, *Lud-in-the-Mist*, (London : Millennium, 2000).

107 Hope Mirrlees, *Lud-in-the-Mist*, (NY : Alfred A. Knopf, 1927), p. 13.

108 Joanna Russ, private correspondence. "The Zanzibar Cat" can be found in her collection, *The Zanzibar Cat* (Arkham House, 1983 ; Baen Books 1984, paperback).

109 I've had the experience of seeing a roomful of non-genre writers burst into delighted laughter when I used this term in reference to them.

110 "Peut-être la mesure de grandeur d'un écrivain est-elle précisément la différence des choses qu'il dit et des choses qu'il sait." Hope Mirrlees, "Quelques aspects de l'art d'Alexis Mikhailovich Remizov" January 15 - March 15, 1926, *Le Journal de Psychologie Normale et Pathologique*, p. 159.

111 Robinson, p. 303.

112 Robinson, p. 304.

113 Morrell Archives, Harry Ransom Humanities Research Center, University of Texas. Excerpts from Mirrlees' letters to Lady Ottoline Morrell are quoted with permission from her literary executors.

114 Woolf, *Diary*, Vol. 3, April 17, 1928, pp. 179-180.

115 Woolf, *Letters*, Vol. III, April 17, 1928, p. 484.

116 Quoted in Hermione Lee, *Virginia Woolf*, (NY : Alfred A. Knopf, 1999), p. 566 ; the letter was dated January 5, 1964.

117 Woolf, *Diary*, Vol. 3, p. 181.

118 *The Times* article, a symposium of notables on the future of marriage, was published July 24, 1926, and reprinted July 11, 2006. The other essays are cited elsewhere in the footnotes and in the bibliography. Given the difficulty of locating them and the serendipitous nature of their discovery, it is entirely possible that more such items are out there somewhere to be found.

119 *Christian Science Monitor*, July 19, 2006 — though I found the article online.

120 This account is taken from unpublished correspondence (none of it by Mirrlees herself) in the A.P. Watt archive at the University of North Carolina at Chapel Hill. At first glance, there seemed to be a small mystery in that the returned contract was for *The Counterplot* and Hope Mirrlees' "next novel," which would have been *Lud-in-the-Mist*. My wife, Marianne Porter, whose former job entailed a great deal of paperwork, however, cleared this up immediately. "Somebody at the publisher's went into the file and grabbed the wrong contract," she said. "It happens all the time." Unfortunately, this means that what might be the sole opportunity to learn the name of Mirrlees' unfinished (and unbegun?) fourth novel was lost. I am extremely grateful to John Kessel for searching through and analyzing these materials for me.

121 Peacock, pp. 246-7.

122 Three years later, the homesick Mirsky was granted permission to return to the USSR. He died in a gulag in 1939.

123 Mortimer, introduction, Mirrlees, *Moods* (Amate Press).

124 It is a sign, perhaps, of progress that this requires annotation. Little Saint Hugh of Lincoln was an eight-year-old in thirteenth-century England whose death was embellished into the blood libel that Jews ritually crucified Christian children and used their blood in the making of matzoh bread.

125 Woolf, *Diary*, Vol. 3, November 30, 1929, p. 268.

126 Morrell Archives, Harry Ransom Humanities Research Center, University of Texas. Quoted by permission of Hope Mirrlees' executors.

127 An unpublished essay by Mirrlees, "The Politic Laird," detailing the peripatetic loyalties of her aristocratic Moncrieff ancestors from Protestant to Catholic and back again as the political climate varied, and their complex intermarriages as well, is in the possession of her nephew, Robin Mirrlees. This may or may not be the same essay mentioned by Catriona Kelly, who wrote, "Finally, in my mother's house there is at least one copy of Hope Mirrlees' pedigree of her mother. It's interesting that she spent so much time writing a history of the family back to the twelfth century (the original ancestors were Spanish — she got this from a published history of the Moncreiffe/Moncreiff/Moncrieff family)."

128 Robin Mirrlees, private correspondence.

129 Catriona Kelly, private correspondence.

130 Robin Mirrlees, private correspondence. This was in the letter later printed in *The New York Review of Science Fiction*.

131 Powell, pp. 180-181.

132 Woolf, *Letters*, Vol. III, January 21, 1928, p. 448.

133 Woolf, *Diary*, Vol. 3, November 30, 1929, p. 268-269.

134 Woolf, *Diary*, Vol. 3, November 12, 1930, p. 333.

135 Woolf, *Diary*, Vol. 4, December 17, 1932, p. 132.

136 Woolf, *Diary*, Vol. 4, June 13, 1933, p. 162.

137 Woolf, *Letters*, Vol. V, November 13, 1934, p. 346.

138 Woolf, *Diary*, Vol. 4, November 21, 1934, p. 263.

139 Woolf, *Diary*, Vol. 4, March 26, 1935, p. 291.

140 Catriona Kelly, however, considers my reading of the photograph "completely inaccurate — she was very formidable, from what I've heard, all her life." In any event, in the wake of Mr. Mirrlees' death in 1923, Hope brought her mother to Paris. Jane wrote to Jessie Stewart that the visit did not "contribute to a quiet & regular life" and that it was "quite clear & very tragic" that "mother & daughter can never make a home together — how little love does towards making compatibility." (Peacock, p. 109 ; letter dated October 20, 1924.) So there is reason to surmise that this earlier arrangement was not the happiest possible situation for either woman.

141 Robinson, p. 302.

142 This book currently resides in the T.S. Eliot Collection in Templeman Library.

143 Quoted in Lyndall Gordon, *T.S. Eliot : an imperfect life*, (NY : W.W. Norton & Co, 1999), pp. 286-7. "There have been numerous memoirs by people who knew Eliot in one way or another," Gordon wrote in his Bibliographical Sources (p. 690). "The best have been cameos which did not venture beyond immediate knowledge. The liveliest came from Hope Mirrlees." The show was *The Mysterious Mr. Eliot : Aspects of T. S. Eliot.*

144 Woolf, *Letters*, Vol. VI, February 10, 1941, p. 472.

145 Mirrlees' papers contain her transcriptions of comments Eliot made to her about poetry and literature; presuming (and it is a presumption) that many of these came from when he stayed at the Shambles, there is a graduate paper to be had for somebody here.

146 "No, that was Hopie who cadged cigarettes!" her nephew exclaimed upon hearing this story. "She'd go on a great remorseful binge when she'd say, 'I'm never going to smoke again.' And then when it got too much, she'd rush out and cadge a cigarette from whoever was closest — Tom Eliot, or the gardener, it didn't matter. She was a great gal for remorse, you see."

147 Gordon, *T.S. Eliot: An Imperfect Life*, (NY : W.W. Norton & Co, 1999), p. 367.

148 According to John Saunders, "Hope's library contained a number of inscriptions from TS Eliot. . . . I found most interesting the inscription on an edition of *Huckleberry Finn* for which Eliot had written the introduction. It read : To H. Hope Mirrlees, in gratitude & affection, who persuaded me to read this book, in 1943." (Private correspondence.)

149 December 7, 1952. This excerpt from an unpublished letter in the Mirrlees Papers at the University of Maryland in College Park is quoted by kind permission of Valerie Eliot, the late poet's widow, who holds the copyright.

150 Robert Sencourt, *T.S. Eliot : a memoir*, (NY: Dodd Mead, 1971), p. 177.

151 Victor Lowe, *Alfred North Whitehead : The Man, His Work*, Volume II : 1910-1947, (Baltimore and London : Johns Hopkins University Press, 1990), p. 29.

152 Eliot's correspondence of the time also expresses sympathy for the strains and stresses that unspecified misfortunes have placed on her. So there may have been even more for her to leave behind than the sorrows of her mother's death. At any rate, she was not happy in England.

153 She lived on the fringes of university life. "There would be people there who remember her," her nephew told me. "She made rather a lot of enemies there, I fear. I have no idea why."

154 Only here and in Sandra Peacock's biography of Jane Harrison is Mrs. Mirrlees' name spelled correctly; all other published sources I have seen refer to her as "Lena." For establishing this small but crucial courtesy and for many other laboriously-obtained details of the Mirrlees family, I am deeply indebted to Lesley Fiedler.

155 Eliot's correspondence with Margot Coker is preserved in the Bodleian Library. I made no effort to examine it for this article, however, since the two sisters were never close.

156 Then again, Hope was not a cook. *Lud-in-the-Mist*, which is rich in herb-lore and antiquarian detail, refers to only four dishes : The Bitter-Sweet Mystery, "a soup of herbs on the successful blending of which the cooks of Lud-in-the-Mist based their reputation" ; The Lottery of Dreams, "which consisted of such deli-

cacies as quail, snails, chicken's liver, plovers' eggs, peacocks' hearts concealed under a mountain of boiled rice" ; True-Love-in-Ashes, "a special way of preparing pigeons" ; and Death's Violets, "an extremely indigestible pudding decorated with sugared violets." Though the names are marvelous, the dishes themselves do not convince. I defy any cook to come up with a recipe for The Lottery of Dreams which would be worth the trouble of its preparation.

157 Hope Mirrlees, *Moods and Tensions : Seventeen Poems*, privately printed, n.d., pp. 10-12. *Contemporary Authors*, vol. 155, p. 340, lists the publication date as c. 1920; this is certainly a typo, given that one poem is dated July, 1961. Janet Saunders, of the University of Maryland at College Park dates this booklet to 1965 (Saunders, "Guide to the Papers of Hope Mirrlees," Archives and Manuscripts Department, University of Maryland at College Park Libraries, December 1993). I have seen two copies of this chapbook, and it is worth nothing that both contain corrections in the author's hand — though different corrections in each case.

158 In 1972, when this poem, along with three others, was reprinted in the first issue of *The Virginia Woolf Quarterly*, apparently at the instigation of Suzanne Henig, it had been retitled "A Doggerel Epitaph for my Little Bitch, Sally."

159 At the time of the Suzanne Henig interview she stated that "she no longer writes poetry and all her time is given over to the second volume of the Cotton biography" (p. 21).

160 Hope Mirrlees, *A Fly In Amber*, (London : Faber and Faber, 1962), p. 102.

161 Hope Mirrlees, "Listening in to the Past," *The Nation & Athenaeum*, September 11, 1926.

162 Margaret Ellis, private correspondence. The typescript of the final draft is lodged with Ms Ellis, as are six boxes of notebooks. She wrote: "Some of these are scrap books, some common place books, some spiritual and religious extracts, and many historical extracts relating to the sixteenth and seventeenth centuries which served as source material for the biography. They are, in general, not indexed, and, as miss Mirrlees was always loathe to waste paper, many are mixed and fragmentary in content. I have found nothing among them to relate to the fourth novel." John Graham Saunders recalls the notebooks as also containing transcriptions of Mirrlees' conversations with Eliot.

163 For a time, she and J. R. R. Tolkien lived within walking distance of each other. As by now seems inevitable, they do not appear to have met.

164 Catriona Kelly, private correspondence. Her mother, (Helen) Margaret Moncrieff Kelly penned a memoir, *Worlds Apart* (UK : Bettany Press, 2003), in which she wrote, "In appearance and manner everything about her was on the largest of scales; and as a teenager I found her distinctly overwhelming, with her loud booming voice and boisterous exaggerated manner. A memory still lingers of Hope, seated at the foot of the wooden staircase in the Shamley Green house, addressing her beloved pug dog, Mary, in tones which rang throughout the house and might have been heard echoing in the farthest corner of the three-acre garden." (Chapter V — "Many Relatives." I can provide no page number, for I've only seen an e-file of the chapter. But, being neither an academic nor dependent on a reputation for scholarly exactitude, I can get along without it.) In that same chapter, Ms. Kelly claimed that *Lud-in-the-Mist* "was serialised by the BBC as recently in the 1980s." According to Louise North, an archives researcher for the BBC, however, there is no evidence to suggest that this is so.

165 Margaret Ellis, private correspondence.

166 John Saunders, private correspondence.

167 Robin Mirrlees, private correspondence.

168 Robin Mirrlees, *NYRSF*. Margaret Ellis noted, however, that Mirrlees "was in a hospital in London for some time with pneumonia in ?1975. She was very severely ill, and used afterwards to date events as 'before' or 'after the flood'!" (Private correspondence.) Fifty years earlier, Virginia Woolf wrote to a friend that Hope "she has some disease, which is always making her ill." (Woolf, *Letters*, 200-201; September 1, 1925)

169 *The Times* (London) recorded that her funeral service was held at Oxford Crematorium on Tuesday August 8th at 2.30 pm.

170 Saunders, private correspondence. Both versions of Mirrlees' last chapbook were dedicated to Lascelles.

BIBLIOGRAPHY & SOURCES :

Peter Ackroyd, *T. S. Eliot : A Life*, NY : Simon and Schuster, 1984.

Mary Beard, *The Invention of Jane Harrison*, Boston : Harvard University Press, 2000.

Quentin Bell, *Virginia Woolf : A Biography*, NY : Harcourt Brace Jovanovich, 1972.

Julia Briggs, private correspondence.

—— "Hope Mirrlees and Continental Modernism", Bonnie Kime Scott, ed., *Gender in Modernism : New Geographies, Complex Intersections*, University of Illinois Press : 2007.

—— "'Printing Hope': Virginia Woolf, Hope Mirrlees, and the Iconic Imagery of *Paris*," Karen V. Kukil, ed., *Woolf in the Real World : Selected Papers from the Thirteenth International Conference on Virginia Woolf*, Clemson, SC: Clemson University Digital Press, 2005.

—— *Reading Virginia Woolf*, Edinburgh : Edinburgh University Press, 2006.

James Davidson, *Secret History*, *The Guardian : Saturday Review*, July 29, 2000 (Quoted in Knitting Circle, a feminist website).

Derek A. Dow, *Redlands House : Hospital, Hostel and Home*, Paisley : Scottish Ambulance Service, 1985.

Charles Du Bos, *Approximations* (4ème série), Paris : R.A. Correa, 1930.

Margaret Ellis, correspondence.

Neil Gaiman, introduction, *Lud-in-the-Mist*, L : Millennium, 2000.

Lyndall Gordon, *Eliot's New Life*, NY : Farrar Straus Giroux, 1988.

Lyndall Gordon, *T.S. Eliot: an imperfect life*, NY : W.W. Norton & Co, 1999.

Jane Ellen Harrison, *Reminiscences of a Student's Life*, L : Hogarth Press, 1925.

Suzanne Henig, "Queen of Lud : Hope Mirrlees," *Virginia Woolf Quarterly* I (1972) : 8-23.

Christopher Isherwood, *Diaries: Volume 1 : 1939-1960*, NY : HarperCollins, 1996.

R. Brimley Johnson, *Some Contemporary Novelists (Women)*, L : Leonard Parsons, 1920.

Catriona Kelly, correspondence.

Margaret Moncrieff Kelly, *Worlds Apart*, Bettany Press, 2003.

Hermione Lee, *Virginia Woolf*, NY : Vintage Books, 1999.

Victor Lowe, *Alfred North Whitehead : The Man, His Work, Volume II 1910-1947*, Baltimore : Johns Hopkins University Press, 1990.

Michael Mirrilees, correspondence.

Hope Mirrlees, *A Fly In Amber*, L : Faber and Faber, 1962.

—— "Bedside Books", *Life & Letters, The London [Miscellany ?]*, v. I (June-December 1928) : 562-574.

—— *The Counterplot*, L : W. Collins Sons & Co., 1924.

—— "Does marriage have a future ?", *The Times*, July 24, 1926, reprinted July 11, 2006.

—— "Gothic Dreams," *The Nation & Athenaeum*, March 3, 1928.

—— "Listening in to the Past," *The Nation & Athenaeum*, September 11, 1926.

—— *Lud-in-the-Mist*, L : W. Collins Sons & Co., 1926.

—— *Madeleine, One of Love's Jansenists*, L: W. Collins Sons & Co., 1919.

—— *Moods and Tensions: Seventeen Poems*, privately printed, 1965. Rev.: Oxford & Tehran : Amate Press, 1976.

—— *Paris : A Poem*, Richmond, Surrey : Hogarth Press, 1919 [i.e., 1920]. 23 pp. (Woolmer 5).

—— *Poems*, Cape Town, South Africa : Gothic Printing, 1963. This publishing information is taken from *Contemporary Authors* (Beard gives its publication date as 1962) ; the extremely plain chapbook itself contains neither year of publication nor publisher's colophon. It looks to be self-published. Perhaps Gothic Printing was simply a local printer.

—— "The Politic Laird," unpublished.

—— "Quelques aspects de l'art d'Alexis Mikhailovich Remizov," *Le Journal de Psychologie Normale et Pathologique*, January 15 - March 15, 1926 Arts and Philosophy issue, pp. 148-159.

—— "The Religion of Women," *The Nation & Athenaeum*, May 28, 1927.

Hope Mirrlees and Jane Ellen Harrison, trans., *The Book of the Bear*, L : Nonesuch, 1926.

—— *The Life of the Archpriest Avvakum, By Himself*, Richmond, Surrey : Hogarth Press, 1929 (Woolmer 41).

Robin Mirrlees, "My Aunt, Hope Mirrlees," *The New York Review of Science Fiction* Issue 163, Vol.14, No. 7 : March 2002.

Robin Mirrlees, correspondence and telephone conversations.

Juliet O'Keefe, " 'Whatever happens, some day it will look beautiful' : Hope Mirrlees's *Paris*". Presented at the Women in Motion Interdisciplinary Conference, May 23-25, 2003, Mount Allison University, Sackville, New Brunswick.

Sandra J. Peacock, *Jane Ellen Harrison: the mask and the self*, New Haven : Yale University Press 1988.

Anthony Powell, *Faces in My Time*, NY : Holt, Rinehart and Winston : 1981.

Annabel Robinson, *The Life and Work of Jane Ellen Harrison*, Oxford : Oxford University Press, 2002.

Jean Paul Sartre, *The War Diaries of Jean-Paul Sartre*, NY : Pantheon Books, 1984.

Janet Saunders, "Guide to the Papers of Hope Mirrlees," Archives and Manuscripts Department, University of Maryland at College Park Libraries, December 1993.

John Graham Saunders, correspondence.

Robert Sencourt: *T.S. Eliot : a memoir*, NY : Dodd Mead, 1971.

Miranda Seymour, *Ottoline Morrell : life on the grand scale*, NY : Farrar Straus & Giroux, 1992.

Alan Sheridan, *Andre Gide : A life in the Present*, Cambridge : Harvard University Press, 1999.

Diana Souhami, *Gertrude & Alice*, L : HarperCollins, 1991.

Jessie G. Stewart, *Jane Ellen Harrison: a portrait from letters*, L : The Merlin Press, 1959.

Alice B. Toklas, *What is Remembered*, NY : Holt, Rinehart and Winston, 1963.

Martha Vicinus, private correspondence.

Virginia Woolf, *The Diary of Virginia Woolf*, Anne Oliver Bell, ed., NY : Harcourt Brace Jovanovich, *Volume One : 1915-1919*, 1977.
— *Volume Two : 1910-1924*, 1978.
— *Volume Three : 1925-1930*, 1980.
— *Volume Four : 1931-1935*, 1982.
— *Volume Five : 1936-1941*, 1984

—— *The Letters of Virginia Woolf*, Nigel Nicolson & Joanne Trautmann, eds., NY : Harcourt Brace Jovanovich.
— *Volume II : 1912-1922*, 1976.
— *Volume III : 1923-1928*, 1978.
— *Volume IV : 1929-1931*, 1979.
— *Volume V : 1932-1935*, 1979.
— *Volume VI : 1936-1941*, 1980.

Howard Woolmer, *A Checklist of the Hogarth Press 1917-1946*, Woolmer/ Brotherson Ltd., 1986

Maria Cândida Zamith and Luísa Flora,, eds., *Virginia Woolf : Three Centenary Celebrations*, Porto : Universidade do Porto, Vaculdade de Letras, 2007.

A LEXICON OF LUD :

the Amber Desert : Amber loomed large in Hope Mirrlees' imagination. Her final book, a rather turgid biography of Sir Bruce Cotton, the Elizabethan antiquarian, was titled *A Fly in Amber*. She wore amber necklaces, and one of a limited number of bequests in her will was a piece of amber with a fly in it. One signifier of the prosperity of Lud is that pigmy pedlars from the far North hawk amber in the streets. See also **flowers-in-amber**.

Appleimp Lane : An imp is the young shoot of a tree, particularly a shoot or slip used in grafting, and thus the lane itself is doubtless lined with grafted trees. But the name has also an allegorical reading. The original "apple imp" was of course Lucifer in the Garden of Eden, and so Appleimp Lane would be the road to Hell. Mirrlees' family were staunch Scottish Covenanters, and the suggestion that damnation lay continually close to hand would fit quite well into her early upbringing.

apricot : The words "it looked like a rotten apricot" appear on the first page of *Lud-in-the-Mist*. A similar image appears in Mirrlees' *Paris : A Poem* originally published by Leonard and Virginia Woolf's Hogarth Press in 1920. "The sky is apricot ;" she wrote, and three lines later, "Flies nibbling the celestial apricot — " implying strongly that it is rotten. Elsewhere, Mother Tibbs says that the fairy fruit is brought in by "All the pretty gentlemen, dressed in green, with their knots of ribands, crowding down in the sunrise from their ships with the scarlet sails to suck the golden apricocks, when all in Lud are fast asleep !" Which seems to identify the apricot as a golden apple, perhaps of the sun. Traditionally, the apricot was used to symbolize female genitalia ("abricot" in medieval France was slang for the vulva), and considered to be an aphrodisiac. Titania included it among the delights proffered Bottom. Whether Mirrlees intended it as such is a matter of speculation. But the association of sweetness with corruption, of foulness with desire, seems clear.

Duke Aubrey : Oberon, obviously, with scandalous hints of Aubrey Beardsley and possibly (given Mirrlees' interest in the Elizabethan era) John Aubrey of *Brief Lives* fame. An Elizabethan poem (see **Willy Wisp**) recorded Oberon's name as "Obrean." Due to his high-handed treatment of the virtue of his subjects' wives and daughters, natural children were referred to as Duke Aubrey's brats.

Duke Aubrey's pack : It is a folk belief in the country districts of Dorimare that "should there be a fairy among the servants, he was bound to return to his own land on one of the twelve nights after the winter solstice ; and should there be among the dogs one that belonged to Duke Aubrey's pack, during these nights he would howl and howl, till he was let out of his kennel, and then vanish into the darkness and never be seen again." So this is explicitly *not* the Wild Hunt. Nat Chanticleer, however, is explicitly identified, though perhaps only metaphorically, as a member of the Duke's pack. See also [**cats, dogs, and birds**].

Aunt Sally : A target in the shape of the head of an old woman with a clay pipe in her mouth, employed in a nineteenth-century fairgrounds game also named Aunt Sally. Players threw sticks in an attempt to break the pipe. Hence, it quickly became a term for somebody who was an easy target for criticism.

Florian and Hyacinth Baldbreeches : "Baldbreeches" was an Elizabethan epithet for a poor man, one who lacked money to buy new trousers when the old were shiny from use. So perhaps the family has in recent centuries risen in estate.

Marjory Beach : The daughter of **Farmer Gibberty's** carter. Marjory is a variant of Margaret, which means "pearl." Which, combined with the spelling of "Beach," means that her name has no botanical component. It's possible the last name was intended to be "Beech"; like many writers, Hope Mirrlees was no great shakes at spelling. Or it may be that countryfolk follow different naming conventions than those in the cities. See also **Diggory Carp.** Then again, it could be an in-joke nod to Sylvia Beach, whom Mirrlees knew.

Bawdy Bess : A "handsome, painted, deaf-mute with bold black eyes." A good cook. She does not appear to have been a procuress, and so the adjective seems to be applied in the sense of filthiness or licentiousness or even in the older sense of being gayly decked-out.

the berries of merciful death : Though the berries are employed merely as a plot device, it is worth noting that the Elizabethans shared a particular horror of poisoning, of which animus Mirrlees, as a scholar of the period, would have been particularly conscious.

blue kine : In Lud, "tradition taught that all the cattle of Fairyland were blue, and that fairy gold turned into dung when it had crossed the border." In Norwegian folklore, a bluish hue is the brand that the hidden people use to mark their cattle. The propensity of fairy gold to turn to dung in the daylight is well documented.

"Busty Brigit !" : An apparent corruption of an earlier invocation to Brigid, Celtic goddess of war.

cantharides : A preparation of crushed blister beetle (*Cantharis vesicatoria*), also known as Spanish fly. In small doses it is, as every schoolboy knows, an aphrodisiac, but in larger doses it is lethal. See also **mercury sublimate, rosalgar,** and **white arsenic.**

Diggory Carp : An unfortunate laborer in the employ of **Farmer Gibberty.** His first name is derived from the French "*égaré*," meaning astray. It is odd that so many of Dorimare's rustics have littoral surnames, when they are situated further inland than the floral Ludites. Perhaps their ancestors once lived proximate to the "great inland sea" of Fairyland. See also **Marjory Beach.**

carminative : The use of this term in one of Mirrlees' many aphorisms, "Let mental suffering be intense enough, and it becomes a sort of carminative," is a sly and unexpected bit of hidden ribaldry. It refers to the medicinal property of relieving colic by inducing flatulence.

catechumen : A person receiving instruction in the basics of Christian dogma with a view to baptism. The use of this term reflects Mirrlees' early interest in Catholicism.

[cats, dogs, and birds] : In Mirrlees' symbology, comparisons to dogs are unfailingly positive and applied only to men. Foremost among whom is Chanticleer, suggesting that he may be, metaphorically at least, one of **Duke Aubrey's pack.** Feline comparisons, however, are always negative and with one exception applied only to women and objects. **Miss Primrose Crabapple** is imagined "screeching like an old love-sick tabby-cat," while "Belling the Cat," the chapter in which **the Widow Gibberty** is arrested, has an extended sequence explicitly equating her with a cat. An apprentice clock-winder fancies the Mayor's clock as his familiar, "a grotesque hobgoblin tabby cat," and when Nat strikes the cock's-head lute and hears **the Note**, one of the girls present characterizes it as a "cat's concert." The only male compared to a cat is **Portunus**, for "the way he always follows about the folk that don't like him." Comparisons to birds, however, are reserved for folks who have been touched by Faerie, most notably **Endymion Leer**, with his "bird-like eyes," and **Nat Chanticleer** himself. In his final peroration, Leer declares that in Faerie birds are dreams.

cere cloths : Waxed cloths, used for wrapping the dead.

Dame Marigold Chanticleer : *née* Vigil. The cheerful yellow marigold has many traditional uses. According to the 1578 translation of Dodoens' *Newe Herball*, a conserve of marigold flowers "cureth the trembling of the heart." With herbs and thyme, it could be made into an unguent that would enable a mortal to see fairies. In a herbal Chanticleer consults, "marygold" flower water is involved in the preparation of an antidote to the **berries of merciful death**. The world "gold" in *Lud* is consistently employed as a signifier of enchantment, both literal and metaphoric, so Dame Chanticleer's first name may well have been meant to alleviate the impression left by her early behavior. As does her maiden name, a vigil being a watchman or custodian, much as the rooster Chanticleer was for his flock. Which fact suggests that she is by nature a particularly good match for Nat and that their troubled marriage is, *à la* Titania and Oberon, a reflection or even a cause of the troubled times.

Nathaniel Chanticleer : Chanticleer (literally, "clear singer") was the generic name for a rooster in Medieval times. In Chaucer's "The Nun's Priest's Tale," Chanticleer, the guardian of his flock, is taken by a fox through his own vanity and lack of vigilance, but cleverly escapes his captor in the end. It helps to understand that Mirrlees employed her own family as a sort of repertory company in her three novels (her first two, *Madeleine, One of Love's Jansenists* and *The Counterplot*, are neither fantasies nor recommended for even the adventurous reader), acting out various roles as needed, sometimes positive and sometimes not, but always identifiable. Nathaniel is, at least in part, Mirrlees' father, William Julius Mirrlees, a wealthy industrialist who had died shortly before the novel was begun, and to whom the book is dedicated.

Prunella Chanticleer : Nat's daughter. "Had a stranger wanted to see an upper class maiden of Lud-in-the-Mist, he would have found a typical specimen in Prunella Chanticleer. She was fair, and plump, and dimpled ; and, as in the case of her mother, the ruthless common sense of her ancestors of the revolution had been trivialized, though not softened, into an equally ruthless sense of humour." The name is rather a cheap shot at Hope Mirrlees' own sister Margot, after whom the character was modeled. The two women were not particularly fond of each other, though Margot may have ended up supporting Hope in her old age.

cheapjack : "Cheap" originally meant to barter, buy or sell ; a cheapjack is simply a vendor.

[Christianity] : Dorimare is torn between the paganism of Fairy and the mercantile humanism of its ruling class. There is only one sentence in the entire novel referring to Christianity : "And when Ranulph had given his eerie scream, Luke had, as instinctively as in similar circumstances a mediaeval papist would have made the sign of the Cross, glanced towards the door to catch a reassuring glimpse of the familiar herb." Note the use of the pejorative "papist." Mirrlees was raised as a Protestant, though she later converted to Catholicism.

churchwarden : Currently, a briar pipe with a short, usually round shank and a very long stem, usually with a long and graceful curve. Ambrose's is more likely to be a clay tavern pipe (or "yard of clay"), such as were common in the seventeenth and eighteenth century. The long stem cools the smoke while simultaneously making it possible to keep the smoke rising from the bowl away from one's face.

cicerone : A guide who conducts visitors to museums or the like and explains matters of archaeological, artistic, or antiquarian interest. The word is almost certainly derived from the learned and eloquent Marcus Tullius Cicero.

the Cinnamon Isles : One of a small number of geographical inventions (the **Amber Desert** is another) which definitively place the novel in an invented world. Lud-in-the-Mist was among the first adult fantasies set in a secondary world with no apparent connection to our own.

cockchafer : A scarabaeid beetle, *Melontha melontha*. Cockchafers are recurrent in *Lud*, and Chanticleer is more than once compared to a cockchafer, buzzing angrily and banging against its own shadow.

Columbine : Not surprisingly, Mirrlees pinched the song. Correctly titled "Fools Song," it's by our old friend Anonymous and was printed in *Robin Goodfellow, commonly called Hob-Goblin, with his mad pranks and merry jests* in 1628 (though the song was probably written before 1600). These words may originally have been performed by jesters at the Tudor court :

> And can a physician make sick men well ?
> And can a magician a fortune divine ?
> Without lily, germander, and sops in wine ?
> With sweetbriar, and bonfire,
> Strawberry-wire and columbine

and :

> Within and out, in and out, round as a ball
> With hither and thither and straight as a line
> With lily. germander. and sops in wine ?
> With sweetbriar, and bonfire,
> Strawberry-wire and columbine
> When Saturn did live there lived no poor
> The king and the beggar with roots did dine
> With lily, germander, and sops in wine,
> With sweetbriar, and bonfire,
> Strawberry-wire and columbine

Mirrlees' sleight-of-hand, putting **Duke Aubrey** in place of Saturn, the god of agriculture and vegetation whose reign was happy, prosperous, peaceful, and virtuous, is suggestive. The verse beginning :

> There are windfalls of dreams, there's a wolf in the stars,
> And Life is a nymph who will never be thine,

so different in phrasing from the rest, and explicitly equating dreams with apples, appears to be original to the book.

Cornflower : One of the **Widow Gibberty's** cows, so named after the unusually blue color of her hide. The cattle of **Fairyland** are blue, and Mirrlees comments on "the strange *moo* of blue cows that was like the cooing of doves," another signifier that when Cornflower inadvertently uncovers the means by which **fairy fruit** are smuggled into Dorimare, she is doing **Duke Aubrey's** will. See also [**cats, dogs, and birds**].

cowslips : The **Widow Gibberty** serves "a great ham with the aromatic flavour of woodsmoke, eaten with pickled cowslips." I have seen it suggested that a cowslip, in this instance, might be a marsh marigold — which would mean that Ranulph has been fed his mother for dinner ! But, unfortunately, the etymology here is false, and pickled cowslips were a common foodstuff among farm folk of the time referenced. **Endymion Lear**, on his rounds, often stops to sample his patients' cake and cowslip wine.

cozener : A cheat, deceiver, swindler, sharper, rook, trickster, fraud, bunko artist, flimflammer, or con-man.

Miss Primrose Crabapple : "Miss Primrose Crabapple had for some twenty years 'finished' the daughters of the leading citizens ; teaching them to sing, to dance, to play the spinet and the harp, to preserve and candy fruit, to wash gauzes and lace, to bone chickens without cutting the back, to model groups of still life in every imaginable plastic material, edible and non-edible — wax, butter, sugar — and to embroider in at least a hundred different stitches — preparing them, in fact, to be one day useful and accomplished wives." Though it is likely that much of her earlier education involved exactly such attainments, it is hard to imagine a fate that Mirrlees, a bluestocking herself, would have welcomed with greater disdain. The witchy qualities of Miss Crabapple are emphasized by her defiant cry in captivity of "Shake me ! Stick pins in me ! Fling me into the Dapple !" The mediaeval witch-finders held that witches when stuck with silver pins did not bleed ; and that when tied and flung into the water, they floated to the surface. It should be noted that the crab apple is not only wild but astringent and sour.

cut the fiddle strings : A common motif in fairy-tales is that of the fiddler, either a fairy or the Devil, whose music cannot be denied. If the music cannot be stopped, the listener will continue to dance until dead, or even longer.

[dancing] : Jane Ellen Harrison, Mirrlees' companion and a famed classicist, theorized that ritual preceded art, and that ecstasy, as in ritual dancing, was the ultimate source of religion, art, and philosophy. The worn shoes left behind by the "Crabapple Blossoms" are evocative of the Grimm Brothers' "The Twelve Dancing Princesses," in which the eponymous princesses go out each night to dance with young men in what is obviously Faerie, leaving holes in their shoes in the morning. Ecstatic dancing played a significant role in Mirlees' first novel, *Madeleine, One of Love's Jansenists*.

Dapple : The river out of Faerie which flows into the Dawl at Lud-in-the-Mist. Its name is typical Mirrleesian wordplay, combining a surface suggestion of a mottled, vari-colored appearance, with a hidden reference to the fairy apples about which the plot revolves.

Dawl : No obvious derivation can be found for the name of Dorimare's mercantile river, the source (until the novel's resolution) of all its wealth, unless it's — but this is a bit of a stretch — meant as a homophone for "dull." In which case, see also **Lud-in-the-Mist**.

Debatable Hills : The "debatable lands" were the borderlands between Scotland and England, contested for by both but firmly held by neither. A soul is not deemed irretrievable until it has passed beyond the Debatable Hills. See also **Elfin Hills, Elfin Marches**.

doited, doitering : Feeble-minded, childish ; applied particularly to the old.

Dorimare : A portmanteau word constructed from sleepy ("dors"), gold ("d'or") and sea ("mare"), particularly apt for a rich, sleepy country by the sea. A dor is also a bum-blebee, an idler, or a **cockchafer**. So the name evokes a threefold hive of gold and buzz and doziness. According to the OED, a "dor-head" is a "blundering fellow," and "dor" itself is "scoff, mockery, 'making game.'" To dor is to befool or mock, which meaning is particularly suggestive given the final paragraph of the novel. Finally, to dor is "to make dim or dull (in colour) ; to deaden." So it may subtly tie into read-ings of **Lud-in-the-Mist** and **the Dawl** as exemplars of dullness.

dragons : Of these beasts, emblematic of fantasy, Mirrlees reported that "there were still a few harmless, effete dragons lurking in caves in out-of-the-way parts of Dorimare."

Duke Aubrey's wooden horse : The gallows. It is perhaps significant that in addition to the legally-sanctioned executions prior to the novel's resolution, Duke Aubrey's jester and **Diggory Carp** also hang themselves, as do so many in the myths connected with Dionysus.

Elfin Hills, Elfin Marches : Though the distinction is fine, these are perhaps not quite the same. The foothills of the **Debatable Hills** are called the Elfin Marches, and assum-ing the Debatable Hills to be identical with the Elfin Hills, then the Marches are a sub-province of them.

Faerie, Fairyland : Used interchangeably, though the first term appears to apply more to the metaphysical state of Faerie, and the second to Fairyland as a physical place.

fennel : In Dorimare, a sprig of fennel is worn on the last night of October to guard against **the Silent People**. Traditionally, boiled in wine, fennel was a cure for snakebite. It was also supposed to be good for the eyesight ; serpents, we are told, rubbed it on their eyes to clear their vision. Hence it is both a protection against glamour (fairy delusion) and closely associated with the Serpent in his dual aspects of devil and wise counselor.

ferret ribbons : Ferret ribbon (or ferret silk, or Italian ferret) was a type of ribbon or tape whose name derived from the Italian *fioretti*, "floss silk." See also **silk**.

Penstemmon Fliperarde : One of the "Crabapple Blossoms," students at **Miss Primrose Crabapple**'s Academy for young ladies. Penstemon or hairy beardtongue was used to make a tea for the relief of female cramps.

flowers-in-amber : A golden eastern wine, of which Master Ambrose's house has the monopoly of import in Dorimare. See **the Amber Desert** for associational value.

fugitives chased by the moon : So far as I can discover, this evocative image is Mirrlees' own, perhaps based indirectly on Harrison's theories. It is presented as a revenant from the deep past of Dorimare, burlesqued in an advertisement for **Moongrass** cheese, "which depicted a comic, fat little man menacing with knife and fork an enormous cheese hanging in the sky like the moon." The original, however, was "a very ancient Dorimarite design, wherein the moon itself pursued a frieze of tragic fugitives." In a very real sense, the Ludites are being pursued by Fantasy itself, whose owlglass emblem is the moon, "Prester John's balloon," as Mirrlees' good friend T. S. Eliot once called it.

fustian : A stout fabric of cotton and flax. Also pompous or bombastic language. The word is used twice in Lud-in-the-Mist, once in each meaning of the word. Given that Luddites euphemize all Fairy matters in terms of cloth, it is telling that Master Ambrose scoffs at a vow he does not realize was once taken by the candidates for initiation into the first degree of the ancient Mysteries of Dorimare, using this word.

"Gammon and spinnage !" : Gammon is a British colloquialism for deceitful nonsense, particularly that of a pretentious nature. The phrase "gammon and spinach," playing on the meaning of gammon as the lower end of a side of bacon, which is often served with spinach, appears, among other places, in the Mother Goose rhyme :

> A frog he would a-wooing go,
> Heigh ho ! says Rowley,
> Whether his mother would let him or no.
> With a rowley, powley, gammon and spinach,
> Heigh ho ! says Anthony Rowley.

"Gammon and spinnage," though rarer, appears twice in the works of Dickens. In *David Copperfield*, Miss Mowcher exclaims, "What a world of gammon and spinnage it is, though, ain't it !"

Farmer Gibberty and widow Clementina Gibberty : A flibbertigibbet is a gossip, a chatterer, and hence flibberty-gibberty means flighty or frivolous. A gibbet, however, is a gallows. While not being programmatic, Gibberty, appropriately enough, carries both associations, with the husband being the posthumous gossip and the widow destined to ride **Duke Aubrey's wooden horse.**

gillyflowers : Properly, *Dianthus caryophyllus*, a fragrant flower used as a spice in the Middle Ages. The gillyflower (or gilliflower, gilver, gillifoure, gelofer, gyllofyr, gilliver, jilliver, gerafloure, gillowflower, or Julyflower) abounds in the poetry of the fifteenth through seventeenth centuries. In its variant spellings, it was applied to a "light-heel'd dame," or wanton, particularly one in the last stage of her good looks, a July flower. Also known as the clove-pink and **sops-in-wine.** In Dorimarite mythology, the dead are carried away by the Fairies to tend their blue kine and reap their fields of gillyflowers. The gillflower is also a variety of apple.

the Golden Apples of the West : In Greek mythology, the three Hesperides, daughters of Night, lived in a garden far to the West of the world, where the chariot horses of the

Sun rested after their long journey across the sky. There Hera planted a golden apple tree which she'd received from Gaia as a wedding gift. Heracles' eleventh labor was to bring back three apples from this tree. Hence they represent the rare, unearthly, and unobtainable. See also, **"By the Sun, Moon, and Stars !"**

the Fields of Grammary : Characterized by Mirrlees as "a picturesque old graveyard on the top of a hill." Grammary or grammarie is an archaic term for "magic," though it originally meant book-learning. When education fell into disrepute during the Middle Ages, familiarity with letters and literature became identified with the forbidden arts. So one of Mirrlees' major themes, the equation of literature and magic is spelled out from the beginning.

Goceline Flack : Goceline is an old English name, but whether it is related to "gosselin" or gosling I cannot say. To flack is to shake something intermittently, specifically to beat with a flail or to rake hay. Thus, although numbered among the cream of society in Lud, Goceline Flack's ancestry, like that of all the mercantile class, is agricultural and humble. All else we know of him is that he owns a dog named Wagtail.

the great drought : Occurring twenty years before the start of the novel, the great drought appears to be the only historical event that the Free State of Dorimare has undergone since the revolution against Duke Aubrey. As Nat jovially observes, "I don't think anything very much happens in Lud, does it ?"

grig : A lively and frolicsome person. A grig can also be a dwarf, a short-legged hen, a species of eel or a young eel, a grasshopper or cricket (from which some derive the phrase "merry as a grig"), a variety of fairy, or a farthing. Samuel Johnson conjectured that the word originally meant "anything below the natural size."

grograine : A coarse fabric of silk and mohair ; also a kind of strong and coarse silk. See **silk**.

hartshorn : The antler of a hart, or deer, used as a source of ammonia and in smelling salts. Salt of hartshorn is a solid carbonate of ammonia obtained by the distillation of shavings of hartshorn or any kind of bone. Spirit of hartshorn is a solution of ammonia in water.

the Harvest of Souls : Though this term is commonly used by missionaries and evangelists in the sense of bringing souls to God, it is more likely that the Ludite usage refers to the Teind of Hell, a tithe that traditionally Faerie pays to its Infernal overlords every seven (or ten) years. But Mirrlees, typically, leaves its meaning ambiguous.

Mistress Polly Hempen : Nat's old nurse, Hempie, has a more significant name than appears at first blush, for hemp is not simply a source of marijuana and the hangman's rope. Fairies were known to wear hempen shirts, and to steal hempen stalks from the field and convert them to horses, which they rode. Hemp is made from the fibers of *Cannabis sativa*, a fact which doubtless contributed to the book's popularity in the counterculture of the early 1970s. See also **Duke Aubrey's horse**. Her first name, being a commonplace for a bird that uncannily speaks with a human voice, marks her as a friend of the fairy-folk.

Luke Hempen : Hempie's grand-nephew, "a lad of about twenty, who worked in the garden and had always been the faithful slave of Ranulph." Luke has the noteworthy distinction, for a Dorimarite, of having a Christian name — and that of one of the Evangelists ! Perhaps it is meant to suggest his moral purity as does the first name of the initially sinister but ultimately solid **Sebastian Thug**. That **Endymion Leer** once went by the name of **Christopher Pugwalker**, however, argues against this. Hempen homespun was emblematic of the rustic.

herm : A boundary marker, frequently with the head of Hermes, Dionysos, or Heracles on top of a square pillar representing the body. Often it had ithyphallic genitalia below, though no such thing is mentioned in *Lud*.

hierophantic : A hierophant, in ancient Greece, was an official expounder of rites of worship or esoteric principles. When the Senators, having donned their official robes, become grave and "even hierophantic" in manner, they are acknowledging that Law has usurped the mysteries of **Duke Aubrey**'s reign.

Ambrose Honeysuckle : Senator, merchant, and ex-Mayor, as well as being Nat's friend. "Amber rose" being hidden in his first name suggests he is of better stuff than he himself suspects.

Dame Jessamine Honeysuckle : "Not without reason, Dame Jessamine was considered the stupidest woman in Lud-in-the-Mist." Jessamine is a form of Jasmine.

Moonlove Honeysuckle : The runagate daughter of **Ambrose** and **Jessamine**. Her first name betrays her ultimate allegiance.

"Ho, ho, *hoh* !" : This laughter identifies **Willy Wisp** (which see) as an avatar of Robin Goodfellow. Similarly, in mediaeval morality plays and Boy Bishop festivals, the Devil sometimes appeared as the clown, with his "devil's bluster" and cry of "Ho ! Ho ! Hoh !"

hornbeam : Shrubs or small trees of the birch family, genus *Carpinus*, with a heavy, hard wood.

in-folio : An infolio is, disappointingly enough, nothing more than an obsolete term for a folio volume.

ivy : Ivy is the badge of the old order. It covers ruined castles and the Guildhall as well, doves roost in it, and peasants place it in their hats as a symbol of disaffection with the current government. It is also, tellingly, emblematic of Dionysus, as well as the holly-god Bran, identified with Cronos or Saturn whose demise was celebrated at Saturnalia, the midwinter festival and whom Mirrlees specifically identified with **Duke Aubrey**. See **Columbine**.

Farmer Jellygreen : Likely a gentle pun, employing "jelly" both in its sense of a foodstuff and as an archaic form of "jolly."

John O' Dreams : Brewer's *Dictionary of Phrase and Fable* defines John-a-Dreams as "a stupid, dreamy fellow, always in a brown study and half asleep." Old John is to be found in Hamlet, in the soliloquy that begins "O, what a rogue and peasant slave am I !" and concludes "the play's the thing/Wherein I'll catch the conscience of the king." The exact lines are :

> Yet I,
> A dull and muddy-mettled rascal, peak,
> Like John-a-dreams, unpregnant of my cause,

And can say nothing ; no, not for a king,
Upon whose property and most dear life
A damn'd defeat was made.

Duke Aubrey's greeting Chanticleer as "old John O' Dreams" is perhaps a gentle taunt
for his not having fully awakened earlier.

"To the King of Moongrass Cheeses !" : Unknowingly, when the merchant princes offer
this toast, they are toasting **Duke Aubrey**'s unnamed and never-mentioned liege and
master.

kittle : Ticklish, emotional.

labyrinth of dreams : When the "Crabapple Blossoms" dance to **Portunus**' tune, they
weave in and out of the labyrinth of dreams. So, too, does **Nathaniel Chanticleer** as
he moves through the novel follow a mazy trail of dreams. He has recurrent dreams
of **the Note**, his son Ranulph converses with otherworldly Powers in his dreams, and
his wife has dreamy and languorous eyes, offset however by the mocking set of her
mouth. In **the Elfin Marches** he is recognized as "Chanticleer the dreamer."

Peregrine Laquer : A member of Lud society who has no active part in the plot of the
book. Lacquer is gold-colored and a peregrine falcon is a bird ; obviously the good
citizen's ancestors owed loyalty to **Duke Aubrey**.

Endymion Leer : A clear reference to John Keats' sonnet, "On Sitting Down to Read King
Lear Once Again," but with the punning element of mockery, suggestive insult, and
malice added. The poem, in its entirety, is as follows :

O golden-tongued Romance with serene lute !
Fair plumed Syren ! Queen of far away !
Leave melodizing on this wintry day,
Shut up thine olden pages, and be mute :
Adieu ! for once again the fierce dispute,
Betwixt damnation and impassion'd clay
Must I burn through ; once more humbly assay
The bitter-sweet of this Shakespearian fruit.
Chief Poet ! and ye clouds of Albion,
Begetters of our deep eternal theme,
When through the old oak forest I am gone,
Let me not wander in a barren dream,
But when I am consumed in the fire,
Give me new Phoenix wings to fly at my desire.

The sonnet implicitly refers to Keats' own *Endymion*, as well as to Shakespeare's play,
rejects Romance for tragedy, and speaks to his own fear of an early death and yearning
for literary immortality. Romance being addressed as a "Syren" refers us back to the
Jane Ellen Harrison epigraph at the beginning of the novel. A tight knot of reference
here. "Hope too well up in the Romantics for my taste," Virginia Woolf once wrote of
Mirrlees, and one can see her point, if not necessarily agree with it. Significantly
enough, he shares a common final syllable with **Nathaniel Chanticleer**.

"lily, germander, and sops in wine" : (see also **Columbine**) In his introduction to the

Fantasy Masterworks edition of *Lud*, Neil Gaiman reports that "The 'lily, germander, and sops in wine' song is first recorded in the seventeenth century under the name of *Robin Good-Fellow or, the Hob-Goblin*." **Sops-in-wine** is a folk name for the **gillyflower**, or carnation.

linsey-woolsey : A coarse fabric woven with a linen warp and a woolen weft. It is warm, durable, and cheap, but not particularly lovely, and hence has become emblematic for poverty. Endymion Leer mentally characterized the Dorimites as this "poor material."

Lud-in-the-Mist : It seems plausible that this name was inspired by love-in-the-mist, *Nigella damascena*, a flowering plant used as filler in bouquets, whose seeds have been variously employed as a hepatic, an astringent, a carminative, an emetic, and in the Middle East as a spice. Even if so, however, Mirrlees' derivation of Lud remains a matter of speculation. Perhaps it comes from King Ludd, the legendary builder of London ? Or as a cheeky shortening of the Luddites, a group doomed as were the Ludites to fight a nebulous opponent against which they could not win ? It may even be the phonetic of "dull" spelled backwards. In which case, see also **Dawl**.

the Lud Yeomanry : "The Yeomanry combined the duties of a garrison with those of a police corps." The implications of this particular usage of "yeomanry" are of a stout-hearted force without pretensions of nobility, of insufficient strength to serve as an army. Adequate, that is to say, to the needs only of a land at peace with itself.

the Lyre of Bones : The most valuable card in the pack used in Dorimare. A folk tale with many variants relates how a murder is revealed when a harp or lyre made from the victim's bones sings of the crime. Thus, the Lyre of Bones represents the ultimate victory of Truth. The "sort of lute ending in the carving of a cock's head," that in the opening pages of the novel darkens Nate's life by sounding **the Note** may be an avatar of the Lyre.

Mab : "The bitch of Rackabite the butcher." Mab was the shortened form of Mabel and also an obsolete term for a slattern or loose woman.

the market of souls : Probably inspired (as indeed was most likely the book) by Christina Rossetti's "Goblin Market," wherein unwholesome fruit, dangerous to the soul is sold to the vulnerable :

> We must not look at goblin men,
> We must not buy their fruits :
> Who knows upon what soil they fed
> Their hungry thirsty roots ?

The sexual subtext (which Rossetti vehemently denied) of "Goblin Market" is to be found only slighter deeper beneath the surface in Mirrlees.

mercury sublimate : Sublimate of mercury was used in Elizabethan times as a bleach and skin-peeler, to hide smallpox scars. In larger doses, it is also a poison. See **cantharides, rosalgar,** and **white arsenic.**

Moongrass : "Moongrass was a village of Dorimare famous for its cheeses — and rightly so, for to look at they were as beautiful as Parian marble veined with jade, and they had to perfection the flavour of all good cheese — that blending of the perfume of meadows with the cleanly stench of the byre." See also **fugitives chased by the moon.**

Mothgreen : A small village, a lovely name, and apparently nothing more.

Mumchance : The captain of the Lud Yeomanry. His name means Silence or Silent or even Tongue-Tied, and is an obsolete Elizabethan term for a masquerade. Mumchance was also a game of chance with dice, in which silence was essential.

negus : A drink named after its inventor, Colonel Francis Negus, representative for Ipswich in the House of Commons from 1717 to 1732. One night, to calm inflamed emotions during a meeting between Whigs and Tories, he heated a bottle of port not quite to boiling, decanted it, and added a bottle of boiling water, two spoons of sugar, cloves, lemon, nutmeg, and brandy.

the Note : The Note is the essence of that song the sirens sang and therefore stands for (as Jane Ellen Harrison put it in a passage which Mirrlees appropriated for the epigraph to *Lud-in-the-Mist*) "the impulses in life as yet immoralised, imperious longings, ecstasies, whether of love or art, or philosophy, magical voices calling to a man from his 'Land of Heart's Desire,' and to which if he hearken it may be that he will return no more — voices, too, which, whether a man sail by or stay to hearken, still sing on." It is the call to transcendence.

opobalsum : The aromatic resinous juice of the *Balsamodendron oposalamum*, more commonly called Balm of Gilead.

orchard thieves : Adam and Eve were the original orchard thieves, and it is worth noting that the fruit they stole was the apple.

patibulary : Of or pertaining to the gallows, and hence hanging, usually employed humorously. Derived from "patible," an obsolete term for a gibbet, a gallows with a projecting arm from which the bodies of criminals were hung in chains and left suspended after their execution, which term is in its term derived from the Latin *patibulum*, a fork-shaped yoke placed on the necks of criminals or a forked-shaped gallows. See also **Duke Aubrey's horse.**

pattens : Various types of footwear, such as wooden shoes, designed to protect the feet from mud or wet.

Peter Pease : The blacksmith in Swan. "Pease" is the plural of "pea," and pease pudding, for those who have always wondered, is simply boiled and mashed peas.

Mistress Ivy Peppercorn : The widowed daughter of **Farmer Gibberty**, and keeper of the village shop at Mothgreen. Her first name being derived from **Duke Aubrey's** emblematic ivy and squills declares her ultimate allegiance from the start.

pigmy Norsemen : Another indicator, like the **Amber Desert** and the **Cinnamon Isles**, that *Lud-in-the-Mist* is set in a secondary world. Mentioned only in passing.

Pimple : The Chanticleers' "little indigo page." Mirrlees unfailingly characterized anyone of African blood as "indigo" and all servants as being of inferior interest, so the dismissive name given him is, alas, no more than to be expected.

pipkin : A small earthen pot.

pleached alley : An alley or lane with tree branches or vines plashed or interwoven overhead. Mirrlees portrayed pleached alleys as a still, quiet halfway state between the mundane world and Faerie. A passage describing how Chanticleer seeks solace in the still quiet of his pleached alley rather sinisterly concludes, "If life in Lud-in-the-Mist could always be like that there would be no need to die."

poncifs : French for "commonplaces" or even "banalities." French was one of eleven languages Mirrlees mastered ; all her life, people commented on her facility with it.

Portunus : Portunes, in British folk mythology, are hob-like creatures who look like old men and often work on human farms. At night, sitting comfortably by the fire, they take little frogs out of their jackets, roast them on the coals, and eat them. They are handy to have about but, like all the fey folk, can prove malicious.

Portunes are surely derived — though no one seems to know how — from Portunus, the Roman god of rivers and seaports, who originally was the god of gates and doors and thus represented with a key in his hand. He is also identified with Janus, the two-faced god of beginnings and of doors, entrances, archways, and bridges. It is in this sense of a "bridge" between life and death, here and there, the menacing present and an uncertain future, that Mirrlees employs him. His muteness (to say nothing of his apparent madness) identifies him as one of **the Silent People**.

Ebeneezor Prim : The clockmaker in Lud, described as "a paragon of dignity and respectability," and used as an indicator of how Chanticleer's social status has fallen when he sends an apprentice to wind Nat's clocks rather than coming himself. The passage of time is inevitable and thus any allegorical reading of a clock-winder would have to acknowledge him as being an personification of Death, of the spirit if not of the body. He has two buxom daughters, Lettice and Rosie, who perhaps became more intimate with **Willy Wisp** than is entirely respectable. Lettice is a variant of Letitia, meaning "joy" or "gladness," and Rosie Prim is, of course, a primrose.

Christopher Pugwalker : One of **Endymion Leer**'s earlier identities. Hope Mirrlees was notorious for owning and doting upon small lap dogs, particularly pugs. The fact that Leer adopted the name of a Christian saint remembered for bearing the child Jesus across a river suggests he himself was or should have been or aspired to be a psychopomp like **Portunus** or a border-crossing prankster like **Willy Wisp.**

purblind : Nearly or half or partially blind. One of Vladimir Nabokov's favorite words.

Ambrosine Pyepowders : The daughter of one of Chanticleer's cronies, and another of the "Crabapple Blossoms." Pyepowders is an obvious variant on Pie-Powders, a reference to the special pie-powders court, or "court of dusty feet," where petty grievances were settled at Medieval fairs. In *Bartholomew Fair*, Ben Johnson wrote : "Many are the yearly enormities of the fair, in whose courts of Pie-Powders I have had the honour during the three days sometimes to sit as judge." Note also that once again an amber rose has been slipped into the narrative.

quinsy : Severe inflammation of the throat ; suppurative tonsillitis.

Hyacinth Quirkscuttle : A weaver long dead before the beginning of the novel. A quirk is a sudden twist or turn, while a scuttle is a basket for sifting or winnowing corn, or for carrying earth, vegetables, coal, etc.

repinings : Fretful discontents, complaints.

riband : Ribbon.

rosalgar : An obsolete variant of realgar, probably chosen for the rose hidden in its name.

(Other occult roses are to be found in **Primrose Crabapple**, **Ambrose Honeysuckle**, **Ambrosine Pyepowders**, and even **Ebeneezor Prim**.) Realgar is a sulfide of arsenic formerly used as a pigment, a medicine, a rat poison, and a coloring agent for fireworks. See also **cantharides, mercury fulminate,** and **white arsenic.**

sherd : A fragment or shard, though the sense in which Mirrlees employs this word — a fragment of fruit — defeats even the OED.

The Silent People : The dead. Also the inhabitants of Fairyland. A Dorimare tradition held that their only means of communication was poetry and music. Hence, in the country poetry and music were called "the language of the Silent People." Not at all coincidentally, *Lud-in-the-Mist* itself is now a tale told by a woman long silent.

[silk] : The very name of fairy fruit being an obscenity in Dorimare, by a legal fiction it was referred to as a form of woven silk. "As above, so below," each thing and action in the mundane world has its counterpart in Faerie. Thus, there are a great many references to woven silk, often incorporating curious or mythic elements from Fairyland, which still retain the power to awe and even terrify those of a receptive disposition. These weavings may therefore represent the domestication of art. See also **ferret silk, grograine, tuftaffity.**

Sops in wine : Yet another name for the **gillyflower**, which see. Also a variety of apple. Joseph T. Shipley, from whose misnamed but delightful *Dictionary of Early English* (in fact, a collection of obsolete words) the entry on gillyflowers is chiefly derived, memorably wrote that "Burroughs in LOCUSTS AND WILD HONEY (1879) states that *bees will suck themselves tipsy upon varieties like the sops-of-wine.* This is hard to believe of the workaday bee ; but I have seen lazy cows apple-tipsy."

Ebeneezor Spike : The baker who, according to his headstone, "having provided the citizens of Lud-in-the-Mist for sixty years with fresh sweet loaves died at the age of eighty-eight surrounded by his sons and grandsons." Ebenezer is Hebrew for "stone of help," and, he being a Dorimarite, the "spike" of his last name would be an ear of wheat.

squills : A small plant with violet-blue flowers. Squills, it seems, are not folkloric. According to Grigson in *The Englishman's Flora*, "Neither the Spring Squill nor the Autumn Squill impressed our forefathers. They are too local, though they wash their blue across acres of sea turf . . . These plants do not produce the squills of the chemist's shop, which come from the foreign Urginea maritima, the true Sea Onion." Which is a pity, because otherwise they would fit so nicely with the healing flora in the book, from the **lily, germander, and sops in wine**, to the **berries of merciful death** and their antidote.

straight white road : The "nymph whom all travellers pursue and none has ever yet caught," is the road to Faerie, specifically identified as the Milky Way. Hence the road of souls, the way of the dead. It is a repeatedly employed in the novel as a metaphor for Truth and for the way to enlightenment. "By the Milky Way !" is a powerful oath in Dorimare.

strawberry-wire : The runner of the strawberry plant and hence by extension the plant itself, or else a long, thin plant-stem very much like a strawberry runner.

"By the Sun, Moon and Stars !" : This oath incorporates all the universe save only the world upon which its swearers abide. Which is to say, all that is not mundane. This specifically references but is not limited to fantasy alone. The single most powerful oath in Dorimare or Faerie is "By the Sun, Moon and Stars, and **the Golden Apples of the West !**"

Swan-on-the-Dapple : A village which Mirrlees characterizes as "a score of houses straggling round a triangle of unreclaimed common, on which grew olives and stunted fruit-trees, and which was used as the village rubbish heap. The name lends the village a glamor which the reality lacks, and if not *quite* a pun, is at least a bit of wordplay.

syllabub : A traditional English desert, consisting chiefly of cream, sugar, and alcohol. Here, modified from an entry in *The Compleat Housewife* (published in colonial America in 1742) is a typical recipe :

Ingredients

2/3 cup dry white wine, 1/3 cup dry sherry, 2 tbs. grated lemon peel, 1/4 cup lemon juice, 2/3 cup sugar, 2 cups heavy cream, sprigs of mint for garnish, assortment of fresh berries for garnish

Instructions

In large bowl, combine wine, sherry, lemon peel and lemon juice. Add sugar until dissolved. Whip cream in a large bowl until it forms medium stiff peaks. Fold into wine mixture.

Spoon into eight wine glasses, cover with plastic wrap and refrigerate overnight. The mixture will separate and be ready to enjoy the next day. Garnish with fresh mint and berries.

In the novel, **Dame Marigold Chanticleer** and **Dame Dreamsweet Vigil** and their cronies periodically gather to eat syllabub and marzipan, exchange new stitches for their samplers, and gossip. For all her antiquarian leanings, this was not a social event designed to meet with the approval of their martini-drinking author.

Sebastian Thug : Smuggler, sailor, and human servant of Faerie. The last name is, if not subtle, at least self-explanatory.

Mother Tibbs : A "half-crazy old washerwoman, who, in spite of her forty summers danced more lightly than any maiden." Which ability marks her as an acolyte of **Duke Aubrey**. Tib is a shortened form of Isabel, and hence a typical name for a woman of the lower classes, as in "Tib and Tom," used in the same sense as "Jack and Jill." Saint Tibb's Eve is the evening of the last day, or the Day of Judgment. There being no such saint in the calendar, an oath to do something by St. Tibb's Eve is a promise it will never be done.

"Toasted Cheese !" : Possibly a corruption of an earlier oath, along the lines of "Cheese and Crackers" for "Jesus Christ." It may also be an oblique reference to the hapless Baker in Lewis Carroll's *The Hunting of the Snark* :

While, for those who preferred a more forcible word,

He had different names from these :

His intimate friends called him "Candle-ends,"

And his enemies "Toasted-cheese."

Tripsand : The Captain of the Yeomanry before Mumchance. I blush to admit I have yet to unravel the riddle of his name.

tuftaffity : A kind of taffeta with a pile or nap arranged in tufts, also known as tuft-taffita. "Barratine" meaning some kind of woven fabric, "barratine tuftaffity" is a redundancy.

the Unicorn : Described as "a low little tavern down by the wharf, of a not very savoury reputation," and "a foul noisy little den." There is a touch of anticipatory irony here in that when, decades later, Ballantine Books published *Lud-in-the-Mist* without bothering to obtain Mirrlees' permission (under copyright law of the times, it had fallen into the American, though not British, public domain), it was published under "the Sign of the Unicorn," the logo for their Adult Fantasy line.

unicorn's horn : The unicorn, being a symbol for Christ, was credited with mystic powers, primary among which was the healing power of its horn. In Medieval times, a drinking cup made of unicorn's horn (most usually, narwhal ivory or rhinoceros horn) was unspeakably valuable, for it was believed to negate the effects of poison. The fact that girls in remote villages applied bits of unicorn's horn to their toothaches is a good indicator of the Dorimarites' trivialization of the mysteries of life and death.

Dame Dreamsweet Vigil : Dame Marigold's sister-in-law. A vigil, as mentioned before, is a watchman or custodian. This, combined with the lady's first name, suggests a long family association with Faerie.

Polydore Vigil : Dame Marigold's brother. The original for this name was Polydore Vergil (1470 ? - 1555 ?), author of *Anglicae historicae libri XXVI* or "English history in 26 books" (1534), the first critical history of England as well as being the first interpretive study of Henry VII, whom he knew. Of him the *Columbia Encyclopedia* writes : "He made use of documentary as well as chronicle sources, and though his critical techniques do not meet modern standards, he marks the beginning of modern English historical criticism."

white arsenic : As_2O_3, arsenious oxide, was employed by women seeking an elegantly pale complexion, who either mixed it with vinegar and chalk and ate it, or else applied it directly to their skin. In larger doses, of course, a poison. (See also **mercury sublimate**.)

White Ladies of the Field : Though they have dwindled in the British Isle to become the ghosts of noblewomen who were murdered and died tragically and now haunt castles or houses, in Germany and Holland, White Ladies were (or are) white-clad female spirits who wandered about swamps, forests, barrows, sometimes aided travelers, were occasionally prophetic, and whose ritual dances (an area of particular interest to Mirrlees) enabled the Earth's fertility.

whitesmith : A worker in "white iron," a tinsmith.

wicker frails : A frail is a kind of basket, woven of rushes, used for packing figs, raisins, or the like. It holds thirty to seventy-five pounds of dried fruit.

wild thyme gin : The pun in the name of this bracing drink is commented upon by characters themselves. The alcohol is described, oddly enough, as a "perfumed grass-green syrup," which sounds more like absinthe than gin.

Willy Wisp : None other than our old friend Robin Goodfellow. An Elizabethan poem, *The mad Pranks and merry Jests of Robin Goodfellow*, records how after making merry with their sweethearts, Robin misled a company of young men returning home over a heath by taking the form of a walking fire. Up and down he led them till daylight, taking his leave with the words :

> Get you home, you merry lads
> Tell your mammies and your dads,
> And all those that news desire,
> How you saw a walking fire.
> Wenches that do smile and lispe,
> Use to call me Willy Wispe.
> If that you but weary be,
> It is sport alone for me.
> Away : unto your houses go,
> And I'll go laughing, *Ho, ho, hoh* !

Robin was the bastard son of Obreon, which is to say Oberon or (in Mirrlees) **Aubrey**, who charged him to do harm to no one but knaves and queans. Of these, luckily, there was no shortage. He went to work for a weaver, but only to bed his master's pretty wife (which casts an interesting light on his stint as apprentice to Ebeneezor Prim, who had two daughters). He went as a fiddler to a wedding, where he doused the candles and kissed the prettiest girls and pinched the others, until he set them all to fighting with each other.

Winckelmann : Johann Joachim Winckelmann was an eighteenth-century German art historian and one of the founders of modern archaeology. His vision of Greek art codified its reception even to this day.

wych-elms : *Ulmus glabra*, a large deciduous tree, growing as tall as forty meters and as old as five hundred years. Because they are susceptible to Dutch elm blight, they are no longer planted. Wych- or witch- as a prefix means "having pliant branches," as in witch-hazel.

Yellow Sand : "White Sand and Grey Sand !" is the proper London street cry. Sand was used to clean kitchen utensils and sprinkled over uncarpeted floors as a protection against dirty footprints. Red sand sold for twopence half-penny a peck, while white sand cost a penny farthing. Yellow sand, however, was Mirlees' invention. Greer Gilman speculates that the color shift was a sly reference to the song Ariel used to lead the shipwrecked Ferdinand to Prospero in *The Tempest*. Which in its entirety goes :

> Come unto these yellow sands,
> And then take hands :
> Curtsied when you have, and kiss'd,
> The wild waves whist,
> Foot it neatly here and there ;
> And, sweet sprites, the burthen bear.
> Hark hark !
> Bow, wow,

The watch-dogs bark ;
Bow, wow,
Hark, hark ! I hear
The strain of strutting chanticleer
Cry, Cock-a-diddle-dow !

Full fathom five thy father lies ;
Of his bones are coral made ;
Those are pearls that were his eyes :
Nothing of him that doth fade,
But doth suffer a sea-change
Into something rich and strange.
Sea-nymphs hourly ring his knell :
Ding-dong.
Hark ! now I hear them — Ding-dong, bell.
Note that Chanticleer puts in a guest appearance in line thirteen.

ACKNOWLEDGMENTS

I would not have been able to write this book without the help, advice, reminiscences, research, and plain hard work of many people, including John Clute, Valerie Eliot, Margaret Ellis, Lesley Fiedler, Neil Gaiman, Greer Gilman, Catriona Kelly, John Kessel, Michael Mirrilees, Robin Mirrlees, Juliet O'Keefe, Marianne Porter, Charlotte Price, Joanna Russ, John Graham Saunders, Martha Vicinus, and the late Julia Briggs. To them and to anybody I may have inadvertently left out, I am most sincerely grateful.